John,

The True Test Is
When No One Sees

We certainly had some times!

Thanks for your friendship

The True Test Is When No One Sees

OBPOS

Robert N. D'Ambola

Scripture quotations marked KJV are from the Holy Bible, King James Version (Authorized Version). First published in 1611. Quoted from the KJV Classic Reference Bible, Copyright © 1983 by The Zondervan Corporation.

Print information available on the last page.

Rev. date: 11/05/2020

To order additional copies of this book, contact:
Xlibris
844-714-8691
www.Xlibris.com
Orders@Xlibris.com
818788

CONTENTS

Blessed are the peacemakers, for they
shall be called the children of God

Mathew 5:9
King James Bible

Foreword

New Jersey's Union County Prosecutor Ruotolo launched the Ethics program years after Serpico made his mark on the NYC. While cops all knew about Ethics, many didn't realize how easy it would be to get caught up in ethical dilemmas. Seemingly harmless situations reviewed in class made even veteran cops think through ethical situations and reevaluate how they dealt with everyday encounters. Now, imagine the challenge of teaching Ethics to crusty veteran city cops, who survived all of their years on the job and never had a problem. Having them consider everyday occurrences that were considered normal, now had to be viewed through a different lens.

Bob D'Ambola weaves ethical dilemmas into classroom discussion that opens the eyes of police recruits and creates an awareness that may have not have been previously considered. It was my honor and privilege to work closely with Bob in this effort. His students were better prepared to survive being a cop due to his thoughtful preparation of class material and his enthusiastic approach to teaching the material.

- Doug Marvin
New Providence Borough Administrator
Retired Chief of Police

Dedication

This book is due to the foresight and commitment of one person. That person would not be me. That person would be Andrew Keogh Ruotolo II. New Jersey Governor, Jim Florio, appointed Mr. Ruotolo to serve as Union County Prosecutor in 1991 following the death of John H. Stamler. Stamler had served as an Elliot Ness type, no-nonsense prosecutor, under both political parties from 1977 up until his battle with cancer ended in 1990. Ruotolo had very big shoes to fill but everyone soon learned they fit Ruotolo as well as Cinderella's slipper fit her after the ball.

Andrew was born November 5, 1952 and grew up in Westfield N.J. He attended Westfield High School and became an All-American swimmer. He graduated Amherst College in 1974 and Fordham University Law School in 1978. He served as an Assistant United States Attorney for the District of New Jersey from 1981 to 1984, working in the Criminal Division.

After his appointment to the Union County Prosecutor's Office, Ruotolo jumped right into the action and began attacking problems, some old and some new. One horrible plight that impacted all races and all socio-economic levels was domestic violence. He wanted to prevent the senseless deaths associated with this crime so he created the Union County Human Relations Commission to combat bias and hate crimes, and established his office's first full-time Domestic Violence Unit as well as the Union County Child Advocacy Center.

Another scourge that infected the County was the proliferation of stolen cars. Newark is the largest city in New Jersey and is located in neighboring Essex County. Car theft was so rampant in Newark that it was named the Car Theft Capital of the World. This epidemic eventually spilled over into Union County. At first the new Prosecutor believed these thefts were executed by professional car thieves who were shipping the vehicles overseas. When he learned that the perpetrators were just youths from the area, taking the cars for joy rides and doing doughnuts (driving in circles melting the tires and creating rings on the pavement) or to commit local crimes, he immediately and drastically changed his strategy.

Ruotolo convened a meeting with detectives from all twenty-one Union County communities and told them he was wrong. It is extremely rare for a politician to admit he is wrong, especially in front of a packed house. He set out a new plan of attack to stop this tidal wave of car thefts.

In 1992 he proposed the Essex-Union County Auto Theft Task Force along with James F. Mulvihill, the Essex County, New Jersey Prosecutor. On the motor vehicle theft problem he said: "You have impoverished youth growing up in a society that measures your value by what kind of car you drive ... these youngsters have the ability to steal expensive cars that they feel gives them instant status in their community ... you give me 100 new jail beds and I'll cut the car theft problem in Newark in half".[1]

The Auto Theft Task Force (ATTF) ran for 19 years, made 3,800 hundred arrests (this included carjackers, armed robbers, and other felons swept up by the ATTF) and recovered $83 million worth of vehicles. This led to a 20 percent reduction in motor vehicle thefts in the Newark, New Jersey metropolitan area. Officers from both counties and Officers from the State Police were assigned to the ATTF for

---

[1]   Wikipedia

various periods of time. They ran an operation that came to be known as The Wolf Pack. Several law enforcement unmarked units would work in a cooperative pack and converge on a confirmed stolen vehicle (the prey) and box it in to minimize the possibility of a high-speed chase thus reducing damages and injuries to law enforcement officers, the suspects, and the general public.

This Task Force became the model for law enforcement agencies around the world to combat rampant auto theft. During my short but eye-opening assignment with the ATTF, we had members from the Israeli Army ride along with us to observe how we did things in good ole' New Jersey. We even appeared in **TIME** magazine. My elbow made it into a picture.

One other problem Ruotolo had the foresight to address, was Police Ethics. He must have seen the storm clouds forming in the distance that would leave many casualties, both civilian and Police Officers alike in its wake. He would have been amazed that law enforcement would become a Presidential campaign issue, that Officers would be ambushed for pure hatred of the badge, that every incident would end up on the evening news, and that Police Officers would be required to wear body cameras to prove their actions were justified because their word no longer held any credibility.

Ruotolo gathered approximately a dozen Officers to go forth and spread his word. These apostles initially instructed Police Ethics all 2,000 Union County law enforcement Officers from all 21 municipalities. After this initial mission was completed, the next phase was to reach all Police recruits before they hit the streets. On December 7, 1998, Prosecutor Ruotolo stated, "Starting with the present recruit class and every recruit class, thereafter, shall have an entire day devoted to Ethics training." This is where my story begins. I along with Chief Doug Marvin of the New Providence Police Department continued instructing Police Ethics for Recruits. I have continued to spread the word of Ruotolo's original mission for over twenty years because I felt it is needed now more than ever.

I did not know Andrew Ruotolo personally but had the honor to be in close proximity of him on several occasions. He was truly a presence when he entered the room. He was what every person wants a leader to be and what every politician wishes they could be. He was handsome, athletic, dynamic, intelligent and truthful. He was destined to move to higher levels of government but that would not be the case. Sadly, like his predecessor, he was diagnosed with cancer in March 1995. He died of esophageal cancer on September 21, 1995 in Westfield, New Jersey. The world never got the chance to know what this loss meant.

I dedicate this book to the memory of Andrew Keogh Ruotolo II.

Introduction

This book is not just for Law Enforcement Officers. It can be applied to any career or any profession. Many times, mistakes in Law Enforcement have much greater consequences than your average civilian job. At the least, they could be career ending with the other end of the spectrum being death, yours or someone else's. We have learned the hard way that there are no Saints among us and that no profession has been spared from bad judgment, fraud, theft, sexual misconduct and every other type of criminal activity.

The Catholic Church has already spent billions of dollars on compensation paid to sexual abuse victims. Across the country, attorneys are scrambling to file a new wave of lawsuits alleging sexual abuse by clergy members, thanks to rules enacted in 15 states that extend or suspend the statute of limitations to allow claims stretching back decades. An Associated Press report found the deluge of suits could surpass anything the nation's clergy sexual abuse crisis has seen before, with potentially more than 5,000 new cases and payouts topping $4 billion.[2]

---

[2] *"New wave of sexual-abuse lawsuits could cost Catholic Church more than $4 billion,"* Associated Press (Dec 2, 2019)

The Boy Scouts of America has filed for bankruptcy, according to a Court document filed in Delaware Bankruptcy Court Tuesday, February 18, 2020. The youth organization, which celebrated its 110th anniversary February 8th, listed liabilities of between $100 million and $500 million and estimated assets of $1 billion to $10 billion. The bankruptcy filing comes at a time when the organization faces hundreds of sexual abuse lawsuits, thousands of alleged abuse victims and dwindling membership numbers.[3] Stop Educator Sexual Abuse Misconduct & Exploitation (SESAME) is an organization that describes itself as a national voice for prevention of abuse by educators and other school employees. It has compiled alarming statistics on the incidences of sexual abuse in schools nationwide, reporting that just under 500 educators were arrested in 2015

- Of children in 8th through 11th grade, about 3.5 million students (nearly 7%) surveyed reported having had physical sexual contact from an adult (most often a teacher or coach). The type of physical contact ranged from unwanted touching of their body, all the way up to sexual intercourse.
- This statistic increases to about 4.5 million children (10%) when it takes other types of sexual misconduct into consideration, such as being shown pornography or being subjected to sexually explicit language or exhibitionism.[4]

According to a recent study by Johns Hopkins, more than 250,000 people in the United States die *every year* because of medical mistakes, making it the third leading cause of death after heart disease and cancer.[5] The third leading cause of death is 100% preventable and yet no one complains about this!

---

[3] Luara Ly, CNN (Feb 18, 2020)

[4] *The Children's Center for Psychiatry, Psychology, & Related Services*, Sexual Abuse *by Teachers is on the Rise* (July,11, 2015)

[5] Vanessa McMains, *"John Hopkins study suggests medical errors are the third-leading cause of death in U.S."* hub.jhu.edu/2016/05/03, (May 3, 2016)

No Politicians can be believed these days even if they are the most upstanding individuals because they are tainted by their colleague's behavior. In 2008 the financial crisis was primarily caused by political deregulation in the financial industry. That permitted banks to engage in hedge fund trading with derivatives. Banks then demanded more mortgages to support the profitable sale of these derivatives that created the financial crisis that led to the Great Recession.[6] Let us not forget that no one went to jail for all of those financial shenanigans and the loss of thousands of private homes. Only Bernard L. Madoff, who lost $50 billion worth of investors' money in a massive pyramid scam, saw the inside of a prison.

This is not Stephen R. Covey's book, *The 7 Habits of Highly Effective People*, nor is it Dale Carnegie's *How to Win Friends and Influence People*. It is a survival book on how to not get fired and save your career and possibly your life. It is common sense based on blunt truth. I picked Law Enforcement as an example because that was my life for almost 28 years. I have known thousands of Law Enforcement Officers, from small Mayberry-size departments, to large County Agencies, to State Police, to Federal Bureaus like the F.B.I., Secret Service, and Federal Air Marshals. Out of those thousands of Officers, I possibly didn't like only a few of them. I would consider that a pretty good ratio. These men and women were the most courageous, patriotic and giving people you could hope to stand next to on that Thin Blue Line, to protect your family and community. A majority of them served out a full career even though it took a physical and mental toll upon them as well as their families. No one walked away unscathed. There were some that totally failed the Ethics Test and it destroyed their career and probably a great deal more. This book is based upon my experience of more than two decades of instructing Ethics to Police Recruits. I began teaching men and women, Xennials, that were young enough to have been my children. I continued with my presentations to classes of Millennials that could now be my grandchildren. I still cannot understand how

---

[6]   Kimberly Amadeo, *"The Great Recession of 2008 Explained with Dates"* the balance.com, (July 01,2020)

they kept getting younger while I remained the same age. Our points of views have drastically changed over the decades. We no longer share the same references and they no longer get my jokes. The attacks on 9/11 took place when the current group of recruits were crawling around in diapers. They were too young to comprehend that terrible time.

This new group of Millennials are nurtured and pampered by parents who didn't want to make the mistakes of the previous generation. Millennials are confident, ambitious, and achievement-oriented. They also have high expectations of their employers, tend to seek new challenges at work, and aren't afraid to question authority.[7] Law Enforcement has now traveled (kicking and screaming) into the technology age, for better or worse. The problems, however, have remained the same or have even gotten more complicated. Stupidity comes in all shapes and sizes. What is worse is that stupidity also lives forever and is passed down from one generation to the next like it's a cherished heirloom. The goal of this course was to end the transmission of the stupid gene.

Many of the examples I used in my class and in this book are based in New Jersey because that's where I grew up, worked, and raised a family. New Jersey, however, does not corner the market on bad decisions or stupid. It was easier for me to collect newspaper articles and track specific data on these incidents. On the contrary, New Jersey Police Officers are among the most intelligent and best trained in the nation. They just screw up the same as anywhere else. I have personally known people caught up in ethical and/or career related disasters. I do not mention specific names in this book if it is not needed to make a point because I am not here to judge the actions by any individual, and they have already been served their own justice and must live with it. You can make your own mind up regarding the outcome of these incidents. I tell my classes it is only a matter of time until their own Department makes the news cycle. Not if, but when.

Before you start reading, I ask two favors of you. The first is that you ignore my apparent chronic (but not terminal) medical condition

---

[7]   Google

referred to as Coprolalia. This is the involuntary (in my case it is intentional) swearing considered to be socially unacceptable, that is unless you have been a cop for way too long. The word does start with "Cop", after all. Some may consider me a professional Vulgarian. I can live with that.

The second favor is that you overlook any incomplete footnotes. I have been collecting information and news articles for over 20 years and I did not think I needed to record exact dates and page numbers where the articles were taken.

I have based my information on numerous media sources. All of this information has been public knowledge, and I have depended on it to be mostly accurate. I understand that reporters go through excruciating pains to ensure that all their materials and information are 100% accurate (oh yes, and I am sarcastic). Please do not blame me for passing on their information or rendition of an event. I'm doing the best with what I have to work with. I had no idea this decades long rant would become a book. I leave you with this quote from George Bernard Shaw – you make up your own mind.

"Those who can, do; those who can't, teach."

**All persons mentioned in this book are
innocent until proven guilty in a court of law.**

Chapter One

The Beginning

"The true test of a man's character is what
he does when no one is watching."

- John Wooden

The "chosen" group of Officers that were selected to instruct the course were required to attend ETHICS TRAIN-THE-TRAINER class. This was a several day course presented by the Southwestern Law Enforcement Institute, Center for Law Enforcement Ethics, based out of Texas[8]. They covered all the major religions and their belief systems. The message was powerful but the delivery system was a difficult one that ran throughout the course. We then had to take this unit of

---

[8]   Formerly known as The Southwestern Legal Foundation, The Center for American and International Law (CAIL) is a prominent international nonprofit educational institution for lawyers, judges and law enforcement professionals located in Plano, Texas.

instruction and boil it down to a five-hour block to fit into our own presentation.

Only law enforcement officers will understand the pain that followed. Law enforcement is not conducive to ANY change no matter how beneficial it may be to the individual or organization as a whole. Seasoned Officers loath mandatory training unless it involves shooting or blowing something up. After all, that is the fun part of the job. Officers grin and bear it when it comes to mandatory training such as First Aid, CPR, and other classes involving *tools of the trade* like RADAR or PR-24. They absolutely hate lectures and being told to change their behavior. We were directed to lecture to classrooms full of change-hating individuals about changing their behavior. What could possibly go wrong?

When veteran officers arrive for an In-Service Class, they only have three questions;

- What time is the first break?
- What time is lunch?
- What time do we get out of here?

That is all they want to know. They do not care what information is jammed in between the start and finish points. To maintain their undivided attention you must do anything, up to, and possibly including, setting yourself on fire.

When computers first arrived on the scene for law enforcement, I attended a lecture and demonstration of this new amazing product that would eventually revolutionize Police Work. The vendor was doing his best to keep his audience engaged while he spoke about the new MDT (mobile data terminal). This laptop would become our future riding partner and instantaneously provide us with all the information we could possible desire.

The salesman went through his entire spiel before he elicited anything remotely close to interest from the crowd. Then he said the magic words. He stated that the computer was ruggedized and could withstand coffee spills and the shock of impact. He held the computer outstretched from his body and stated, "I could drop this unit and nothing will happen to it".

You cannot make a claim like that in front of a room full of cops without proving it. Even the guy that perfected bulletproof vests had to eventually shoot himself to prove his point. The audience stopped the salesman in his tracks and yelled, "Go Ahead." He did not, or could not, comprehend what they had said. They repeated with further explanation, "Go Ahead, Drop It." He totally boxed himself into a corner from which there was no escape. He only had one recourse and that was to allow his very expensive new piece of technology to slip from his grasp and plummet to the hardwood stage floor. It was worth the trip just to watch his face contort as the computer impacted. It didn't explode into pieces as the crowd had hoped, but we never learned if it ever turned on again.

The bloodthirsty, torch bearing villagers was satisfied and only had one follow-up question for the vendor after that demo. Someone yelled out, "How much?" Because money always runs the show. Once again, he had no choice but to answer the very direct question. When he announced the cost of the system was $100,000 (in 1980s dollars), the entire audience immediately got up and left, leaving him standing there alone on the stage. That day the vendor learned never again to present to a mob of police officers. He would be better off doing his dog and pony show for the sole administrator alone in his office.

My presentation to veteran Officers turned out to be even more painful than the computer salesman's experience. The only saving grace was that I had a co-instructor for support and knew that I would not die alone. The classes were held at the Police Academy in rooms that accommodated 40 to 50 Officers. These Officers were either rescheduled for this class instead of working their regular shift or were on their day off. Either way they would rather have been somewhere else. Anywhere else. We quickly disposed of the obligatory three questions and began our instruction. We were immediately met by extremely blank stares and a lot of heavy sighs. This was going to be a very long day.

The mood of the class was clearly reflected in a quote by Konstantin Josef Jireček.[9] "We, the unwilling, led by the unknowing, are doing the impossible for the ungrateful. We have done so much, for so long, with so little, we are now qualified to do anything with nothing." And we were going to tell these Officers something they didn't know.

The two of us had to immediately breakdown any barrier that gave the impression we were better than anyone else in the class. We were not. But that still did not ease the tension in the room, and we were met with what comedians referred to as extreme heckling. Again, these were seasoned Officers and were not shy to speak up regarding their displeasure. We could easily read their minds and knew they were thinking, "who the fuck are you to tell us that we need to be more ethical." It was not our intention to school these Officers about taking a free cup of coffee.

My co-instructor, Cranford Police Lt. Steve Wilde, and I knew it was more than that. We fully understood the consequences that an Officer could face if he or she got into a jam. It just so happened that a few days prior to this first class, a local Police Officer had shot himself to death in October of 1998. The Officer was a recent Persian Gulf war veteran and had been arrested for shoplifting[10]. To add insult to injury, he was arrested by fellow Officers from his own Department. Prior to the arrest he had been planning on taking the test for Sergeant and was happy with his life. The Officer had been working off-duty security at a drugstore and was seen concealing merchandise under his car. He was released after his arrest and suspended without pay pending the outcome of criminal charges and an internal disciplinary hearing. It could have been something he could have easily survived.

9   Wikipedia, Konstantin Josef Jireček[a] (24 July 1854 – 10 January 1918) was an Austro-Hungarian Czech historian, politician, diplomat, and Slavist. He was the founder of Bohemian Balkanology (or Balkan Studies) and Byzantine studies, and wrote extensively on Bulgarian and Serbian history. Jireček was also a minister in the government of the Principality of Bulgaria for a couple of years.
10   Elizabeth Moore & Jennifer Golson, *"Accused officer an apparent suicide,"* The Star Ledger (1998).

When the much anticipated first break came around, an older Lieutenant approached me and told me the deceased Officer had worked for his Department. He stated that they (The Department) were not going to give him a Police funeral at first, but the Officer *did the right thing*. The Officer had rented a motel room and had laid out his dress military uniform along with all his awards and medals. He then shot himself in that room. I stood there horrified as the Lieutenant spoke these words to me, "did the right thing!" I couldn't believe that he thought this was the right thing to do. I could not comprehend going to a supervisor, or anyone for that matter, and asking for advice regarding such a serious problem and hearing his answer was I should kill myself. At this moment I realized that this class was far more important than I ever thought it could be. I also had no idea what lurked beneath the surface of this senior Officer.

At that time, that Lieutenant was one of the most influential Officers in the Elizabeth Police Department. A grand jury report in 1998 said that nearly one-fifth of the 370-member force belonged to a secretive and disruptive group of Officers known as The Family. Officers on the force had testified under oath that the group, led by the Lieutenant, conducted bizarre initiation and excommunication rituals.[11] That would be revealed at a much later time. I was not going to reach a person like the dinosaur that stood in front of me but maybe there was hope for a younger Officer.

For months that passed as dog-years, Steve and I, along with the rest of the team continued to instruct every excruciating in-service class until we had completed talking to all 2,000 Police Officers in Union County. We were yawned at, dismissed, and ignored. I believe there may have been gassed passed in our direction. We all were very lucky not to have been shot at. Sometimes a couple of Officers paid attention to us. Every day, new articles continued to appear in the *Star-Ledger* reporting on some Officer somewhere getting into trouble, often brought on by their own doing. Our mission had just begun.

---

[11]   Chris Hedges, *"Blue Shadows – A special report: Suspicions Swirl Around New Jersey Police Clique," Zygon:* The New York Times Sec A Pg. 1 (May 13, 2000).

Chapter Two

Reprieve

"The bravest are surely those who have the clearest
vision of what is before them, glory and danger alike,
and yet notwithstanding go out to meet it."

- Thucydides
Athenian General

There was a light at the end of the proverbial tunnel to end this suffering and this time it wasn't the train hurtling towards me. The light took the form of new hope. Prosecutor Ruotolo wanted to expand his goal and reach the newbies, those raw recruits still in the Police Academy, who had not yet been tainted by life's experiences. Ruotolo may have been a fan of the 1987 movie, *The Untouchables*. There was a scene where veteran Chicago cop, Jim Malone (Sean Connery) explains to Elliot Ness (Kevin Costner), "If you're afraid of getting a rotten apple, don't go to the barrel. Get it off the tree."

This time we were headed to the orchard. I had a new partner to co-instruct along with me. It was Lt. Doug Marvin from neighboring New Providence Police Department. We were the only two left out of the original apostles that had agreed to stay on for this second phase instructing the recruit class. Doug and I had been friends for at least twenty years by the time we were partnered up for this mission. He was the perfect match for me as he was everything I was not. He was calm, well-spoken, professional, easy going and well mannered. He was even taller. I, on the other hand, had a similar approach to teaching as comedian, Sam Kinison,[12] minus the blood curdling scream, portrayed in the movie *Back to School.* Doug reeled me in when I strayed a tad too far, which was often. He was my Zen Master.

Let me just say that I hold the instructors from the Southwestern Law Enforcement Institute, Center for Law Enforcement Ethics in very high regard. I meant no disrespect when I adapted their course to fit into a format that I felt more comfortable. I have, let's say, a *different* approach in my method of instruction. Doug and I were presenting a popcorn-fart dry subject to a bunch or green recruits that thought they signed up for wild car chases and shoot-outs with bad guys. They had to undergo twenty weeks of basic training only to be told at the end of their journey they didn't know shit by their assigned Department Training Officer. It would take at least another six months for them to be able to find their ass with both hands and another year, at minimum, to have the slightest clue as to what they were doing. The Recruit day started at around 0400 hours (4am) with vigorous PT (Physical Training) and, yes, a lot of screaming and hollering in their face for not knowing their right foot from their left when marching.

By the time we got these bodies in their seats to begin class at 0900 hours, they were totally exhausted. The last thing they wanted to do was to keep their eyes open one more minute, never mind five more hours, and listen to us spew out what we believed to be words of

---

[12] Samuel Burl Kinison (/ˈkɪnɪsən/; December 8, 1953 – April 10, 1992) was an American stand-up comedian and actor. A former Pentecostal preacher, he performed stand-up routines that were characterized by an intense style, similar to charismatic preachers, and punctuated by his distinct scream.

incredible wisdom. The good news for us was that, unlike the cranky, hardcore, grizzled, veteran cops, that wanted to end our careers, if not our lives, these recruits were unarmed and absolutely had to listen to us. One perk to instructing the class was the recruits were required to snap to attention when an instructor entered the room. There was also a lot of "Siring" going on which I totally ate up. Forced respect is not a bad thing as I never received it back at my own Department. For God's sake, Lt. Marvin's Officers, from another Department treated me better than my own Officers and they had no obligation to do so.

My purpose for changing the curriculum was to maintain their interest, keep them engaged for the entire class (5-hour day at that time), make it bearable, prevent them from smashing their foreheads into their desks due to intolerable boredom, have a little fun, and maybe have a few things sink into their, "I-already-know-everything" brain. I did not want to live with the thought of a young cop shooting him or herself because they screwed up. I knew I couldn't save them all from terminal stupidity, but I was going to try to save as many as I could.

Chapter Three

The Pile

"Service to others is the rent you pay for your room in Heaven"

- Muhammad Ali

My introduction to the class was, let's say, slightly unorthodox. I began with acknowledging the current climate of the time. People were more sensitive about just about everything. I wanted to reassure the class that if I, in any manner, offended anyone at any time during the presentation, that it was too fucking bad. I explained that I was Hello Kitty compared to the people they would run into out on the street. Actually, the worst people they would meet would turn out to be some of their own bosses. You expected to take shit from the bad guys. It was a harsh reality when it comes from someone you were supposed to trust and respect.

I then told the group that I was a professional curmudgeon, or in terms that may be more familiar, an old grouchy fart. I was proud of my curmudgeny, because I had earned every ounce of it and had the pain to show for it. I followed up this statement with another blow direct to the solar plexus.

I told them I hated everyone, most especially, everyone in the room. It was not personal. It was pure jealousy on my part. These young recruits were about to begin the best career that they would ever hate. They would complain about it every day starting from the basic training they were now submerged in up to their necks like life-sucking quicksand. They would complain about the job every day they went out on patrol, and they would complain about it when they walked out the door after they retired. If they did it right, they wouldn't have it any other way. I began the class.

I needed an attention grabber that would kick off the start of the class. I found my answer in a short clip from the 1993 movie, *Jurassic Park*. In Steven Spielberg's massive blockbuster, paleontologists Alan Grant (Sam Neill), Ellie Sattler (Laura Dern) and mathematician Ian Malcolm (Jeff Goldblum) are among a select group chosen to tour an island theme park populated by dinosaurs created from prehistoric DNA. While the park's mastermind, billionaire John Hammond (Richard Attenborough), assures everyone that the facility is safe, they find out otherwise when various ferocious predators break free and go on the hunt.[13]

To this day I have no idea why Alan Grant selected Dr. Malcom to check out the island. He was a mathematician! Anyway, he assisted Ellie in her search for the reason why the Triceratops they came across became ill. The answer, she believed, could be found within the pile of dinosaur droppings. When Dr. Malcolm comes upon a massive load of dung, he exclaims, "That is one big pile of shit." I then shut off the recording (on the original VHS tape) and turned to the class to tell them that that was the entire class and thanked them for coming.

"One Big Pile of Shit" (OBPOS) became my mantra. My explanation, however distorted, is as follows: I explained that, Dr. Malcolm, although not being an expert on dinosaurs, had no problem recognizing one big pile of shit when he saw one. I tried to appeal to the

---

[13]   Google

recruits that they themselves must learn to recognize their particular pile of shit, that may appear in their path at any given moment, and avoid it, if at all possible. The world of Law Enforcement does not always afford you this option of avoidance.

More often than not, officers are dispatched to an incident or complaint that quickly escalates into one big pile of shit waiting to happen. This is the nature of the beast. A perfect example of the OBPOS scenario is the Eric Gardner tragedy.

> On July 17, 2014, Eric Garner died in the New York City borough of Staten Island after Daniel Pantaleo, a New York City Police Department (NYPD) officer, put him in a chokehold while arresting him. Video footage of the incident generated widespread national attention and raised questions about the appropriate use of force by law enforcement.

> NYPD officers approached Garner on July 17th on suspicion of selling single cigarettes from packs without tax stamps. After Garner told the police that he was tired of being harassed and that he was not selling cigarettes, the officers attempted to arrest Garner. When Officer Pantaleo placed his hands upon Garner, Garner refused to cooperate and pulled his arms away. Pantaleo then placed his arm around Garner's neck and wrestled him to the ground. With multiple officers restraining him, Garner repeated the words "I can't breathe" 11 times while lying face down on the sidewalk. After Garner lost consciousness, officers turned him onto his side to ease his breathing. Garner remained lying on the sidewalk for seven minutes while the officers waited for an ambulance to arrive. Garner was pronounced dead at an area hospital approximately one hour later. Officer Pantaleo was placed on desk duty following Garner's death.

The medical examiner ruled Garner's death a homicide. (According to the medical examiner's definition, a homicide is a death caused by the intentional actions of another person or persons; the use of the term does not necessarily mean that a crime was committed.) Specifically, an autopsy indicated that Garner's death resulted from "[compression] of neck (chokehold), compression of chest and prone positioning during physical restraint by police". Asthma, heart disease, and obesity were cited as contributing factors.

On December 3, 2014, a Richmond County grand jury decided not to indict Officer Pantaleo. This decision stirred public protests and rallies, with charges of police brutality made by protesters. By December 28, 2014, at least 50 demonstrations had been held nationwide in response to the Garner case, while hundreds of demonstrations against general police brutality counted Garner as a focal point. On July 13, 2015, an out-of-court settlement was announced in which the City of New York would pay the Garner family $5.9 million. In 2019, the U.S. Department of Justice declined to bring criminal charges against Pantaleo under Federal Civil Rights Laws. A New York Police Department disciplinary hearing regarding Pantaleo's treatment of Garner was held in the summer of 2019; on August 2, 2019, an Administrative Judge recommended that Pantaleo's employment be terminated. Pantaleo was fired on August 19, 2019, five years and one month after Garner's death.[14]

This tragedy occurred after a citizen complaint was filed with Police regarding a minor offense, the selling of single untaxed cigarettes. Can

---

[14]   Wikpedia

you think of anything less important to lose a life over? I have seen hundreds of arrests and most of them were not pretty. No one ever died during any arrest I participated in. Was this because every rule was followed and every procedure strictly adhered to? Of course not, because rules and procedures go out the window in many cases due to the shear insane nature of the goal trying to be accomplished. The reason no one died during the arrests I participated in was because my fellow officers and I got damn lucky, as did the suspects.

If you watch the video of this arrest (because it's on the internet) it shows nothing out of the ordinary. Police approach Garner, he resists the officers slightly, they overwhelm him to gain control, because he is a large individual. They slowly take him down to the ground, Gardner dies. There were no punches thrown or violent action by either Garner or the officers. What was in dispute was the 'chokehold' that Officer Pantaleo applied.

I am not here to pass judgment on anyone's actions. Sometimes things go bad quickly. There were a hundred shoulda, coulda, wouldas that did not take place that day. Did Gardner have the slightest notion he was going to die that day? Probably not. Did Officer Pantalea think his actions would result in the death of a total stranger? Probably not. Do the Police ever want to purposely or accidentally kill anyone? Absolutely not. Police shoot and kill approximately 1,000 people per year.[15] Do some people believe that Police want to kill anyone not actively trying to kill them? Absolutely. There lies the problem. If you haven't stood in a Police Officer's shoes, then you have no idea what shit hitting the fan truly means.

One year after the Garner tragedy the NYPD changed to a new program of *Community Policing*. They were stepping away from the, racially charged, *Stop & Frisk Policy*, of the Bloomberg days.[16] It's ironic that the article quoted here, mentions Eric Garner and Stop & Frisk in the same breath. Eric Garner was not racially profiled nor was he

---

[15] The Washington Post (Feb 26, 2020)

[16] Editorial, One year after 'I can't breathe,' a gentler NYPD?, The Star Ledger (2015) pg. 7

stopped and frisked. The media does not care about these details. Police responded to a citizen complaint. The media constructs the scenario to fit their agenda. I will follow up with both of these topics later on. On Friday, June 12, 2020, Governor Cuomo signed the Eric Garner Anti-Chokehold Act into law, making it a felony in New York for an Officer to engage in a chokehold – except in situations where they are protecting their own life.[17]

The Eric Garner incident is replayed thousands of times every day across America involving numerous circumstances, races, age groups, and genders with a wide variety of results. The Big Pile of Shit that most often impacts the police with horrendous consequences is often self-inflicted. The following is a true story passed down from the Southwestern Law Enforcement Institute instructors. It originates out of California. I call it...

The Fish Story

A wife pulls into her driveway after returning from a shopping trip with her kids in the backseat. She activates the garage door opener and waits patiently as the door slowly rises. As the door completes its journey up the track, a horrific scene appears before her. Her husband had hung himself in the garage. She quickly ushers her children into the house and calls the police. The Police respond and go about their usual routine to handle the situation. In such cases the body is often left, as is, after determining the person is dead. This is so the investigative team and Medical Examiner can observe the original scene undisturbed. It usually takes some time for these back-up units to arrive. It is not a pleasant job to babysit a corpse so the task is usually assigned to the FNG (Fucking New Guys).

Police Officers have a very short attention span on par with a five-year old, and get bored quickly. A wise man once said, "Boredom is the mother of stupidity" oh wait, that was me that said that. Watching a

---

[17] Avalon Zoppo, *"Protests 'necessary', Eric Garner's mother says"* The STAR LEDGER, (June 15, 2020), Pg. A5

dead guy quickly falls into the boredom category. Police Officers are also inquisitive by nature so they started looking around the garage. One new Officer finds that the deceased was an avid fisherman. The Officer discovered a quantity of deep-sea fishing gear in the corner of the garage. It doesn't take him long to come up with a brilliant idea. He grabs one pole and walks up to the suspended person and holds the fishing rod out to his side as if he were posing with a prized sailfish that he had just caught. The second Officer, finding this totally hilarious, runs out to the patrol car to retrieve a Polaroid camera to instantly document this genius. They take several pictures taking turns posing with the body. There is an unwritten rule in law enforcement that you must document your stupidity.

When they return to Police Headquarters, they immediately share the pictures with their fellow Officers. The second unwritten rule states that you must share your stupidity. The two young Officers become instant legends as the story of their fishing trip spreads. Everyone thinks that this is incredibly funny that is, until the wife finds out! Ben Franklin said, "Three people can keep a secret if two of them are dead." This stupidity was destined to get out.

The term most often used to describe these Officers is either "former" or EX Police Officers. This will be recurring terms throughout this book. There was no way they were going to explain their way out of this insensitive stupidity. That was one big pile of shit that they should have seen coming, brought upon themselves, and they made sure it was spread around so everyone knew they were stupid. The administration happily agreed.

You don't have to be a paleontologist to recognize a big pile of shit. The piles are all over the place like landmines. Sometimes you respond to them, and sometimes you create them yourself. Sometimes the Mayor, Chief, or your immediate supervisor throw you into one head first, and sometimes it's you best friend or partner. There are times when you don't have to actually step in one to be impacted by it. Often it is enough just to be in close proximity to the pile to get enough smell on you to make you stink. Many times, that stink will linger for up to five years in court proceedings, as shown in the Garner incident, and then there are times when that stink can never be removed. They call that being in the wrong place at the wrong time.

You can make just one mistake
And it can take you to your grave, honey
One bad move can turn your world upside down
It's such a shame 'cause you've been so good up to now

-Lyle Lovett

OBPOS comes in a variety of shapes and sizes. There are times when you do the right thing and everything turns to shit right before your eyes. (Eric Garner + chokehold)) There are times that stupidity plays a major role in the Officer's behavior (see The Fish Story). There are other situations where the Officer is plain wrong and continues to make things worse. And then there is just plain criminal activity that is clearly prohibited. The last category should not be included in Ethics because it is criminal and out of bounds of Police procedure, but I shall provide some examples anyway.

* **Author's Note:** As I have stated, One Big Pile of Shit (OBPOS) had become my mantra. I had the recruits repeat it loud and clear and told them if they did not come away from the class with anything else, they needed to remember that slogan. These instructions had unintended consequences. My son is a Police Officer and I had the extreme pleasure of embarrassing him (required dad job) in one of these very same recruit classes. Fast forward several months, the two of us were going into a movie and his cell phone rang. The caller was another Police Officer who had been in the recruit class with my son. My son tells the caller he is out with his dad. The caller replied, "Oh, One Big Pile of Shit." That is not how I wish to be remembered.

Chapter Four

The Inverted Asshole Triangle

"When the sphincter gets tighter, vision gets narrower."

-Unknown

You are going to have to trust me on this one and hang in there for a bit for me to go around the corner to get to the point of this gem. Law Enforcement changes you in many ways, physically as well as mentally. I will get to the other ways later on. For now, I will focus on perception. Perception is a vital component to decision making. It is the manner in which a person becomes aware of something by using all of their senses and then processing the information instantaneously to arrive at a conclusion. The ultimate goal is to get to the correct conclusion.

When a person is a new Police Officer there is a universal basic understanding of good guy vs. bad guy. All criminals are assholes.

- All criminals

After a short period of time on the job, Officers see the carnage that drunk drivers leave in their wake involving, accidents, injuries, and sometimes the death of innocent persons. Drunks are often rude and abusive and sometimes they puke in your car and you have to clean it. You see them as a nuisance and a waste of skin. Drunk drivers are assholes.

- All criminals
- Drunk drivers

Patrol duty involves countless hours of driving around at all times of the day and night. You come across thousands of horrible drivers over the course of the years. Many of them drive this way on purpose. They are all a menace to society and you regret not being able to catch them all. Reckless drivers are assholes.

- All criminals
- Drunk drivers
- Reckless drivers

Eventually these people who can't drive have to get out of their vehicles. They then demonstrate to everyone that they also can't park. They block fire hydrants and driveways. They either park on a sidewalk or in the middle of the street obstructing traffic. You dream of owning a fleet of tow trucks that you would operate 24 hours a day to drag these vehicles away to be crushed into small blocks of metal. People who can't park are assholes.

- All criminals
- Drunk drivers
- Reckless drivers
- People that can't park

It takes maybe a year of being around cops to understand that not being around cops is not as much fun. *Civilians* don't get it. They have no idea what you do or why you do it but are professed experts because they watch television. The public does not understand that arresting someone is an adrenaline pump, especially after you have to chase them down. They think you a stormtrooper if they get pulled over for going through a stop sign. Yes, that's what stormtroopers did in Nazi Germany. Civilians are clueless about guns, and they certainly don't get The Fish Story. Anyone that isn't a cop is an asshole.

- All criminals
- Drunk drivers
- Reckless drivers
- People that can't park
- Anyone that isn't a cop

The Chief is a pain in my ass. Does he stay awake at night thinking of stupid shit for us to do? He has not been a REAL cop for a hundred years. Now he is just a fucking pencil pushing puppet of the Mayor. When the hell is he going to retire? The Chief is an asshole. At this point in the class I appointed a volunteer to walk into the Chief of the Academy's office and ask him if he is indeed an asshole. The poor recruit almost has a movement in his or her pants. They remain frozen and look me in the eye and say, "No sir, I can't do that sir." It is these moments I live for (because I am an asshole). After a few uncomfortable minutes I let them return to their seat. They exhale loudly. If by chance the Chief wandered into my class at some point after that beautiful moment, I would announce to him, "Chief, this recruit has a question for you." You could capture the scent of terror coming from the recruit in a bottle. Had the recruit possessed a set of cast iron balls or been insane enough to take me up on my offer, I had prearranged it with Chief Eric Mason*, Director of the Academy, so as not to get the recruit ejected from the class for insubordination. In twenty years, no one had met either of those requirements. When the Chief did come into the room, he would readily admit that he was in fact an asshole.

- All criminals
- Drunk drivers
- Reckless drivers
- People that can't park
- Anyone that isn't a cop
- The Chief

I understand the Chief being an asshole, but my Sergeant is still a cop, and he is almost as bad. He is supposed to have my back but instead is always riding it. Stay on post, wear your hat, write some tickets, clean your uniform! What the fuck, I could have stayed home and listened to my mother yell at me. My Sergeant is an asshole.

- All criminals
- Drunk drivers
- Reckless drivers
- People that can't park
- Anyone that isn't a cop
- The Chief
- My Sergeant

Every time I get in the patrol car is smells like shit. It's full of garbage, the equipment is missing and there are never any reports. Who the fuck leaves their stinky ass tobacco chew spit cup behind? It takes me twenty minutes to clean the damn thing out and do these guys even know what a car wash is? All the other cops that are not on my shift are assholes.

- All criminals
- Drunk drivers

- Reckless drivers
- People that can't park
- Anyone that isn't a cop
- The Chief
- My Sergeant
- All the other cops that are not on my shift

The only person I can count on is my partner. We have been together through thick and thin. We have saved each other on numerous occasions. We are like family, no, closer than family because we would die for each other if we had to. Everyone but my partner is an asshole

- All criminals
- Drunk drivers
- Reckless drivers
- People that can't park
- Anyone that isn't a cop
- The Chief
- My Sergeant
- All the other cops that are not on my shift
- Everyone but my partner

You know lately

- All criminals
- Drunk drivers
- Reckless drivers
- People that can't park
- Anyone that isn't a cop
- The Chief
- My Sergeant
- All the other cops that are not on my shift
- Everyone but my partner
- HE'S STARTING TO ACT LIKE AN ASSHOLE

No matter who you are or where you are in life, if you get to the point that everyone else is the problem, you need to take a deep breath and reassess. The problem is you.

Yes, I have been and continue to be an asshole. Now I am more cognizant of an approaching asshole moment and try harder to avoid it, unless the person I'm dealing with is an asshole, and deserves the same treatment returned. During my class I am a condescending asshole to the recruits. I am fully aware of this and try to do it in a humorous manner. Due to their age, I often stop in mid-sentence to explain what I am talking about. I will define what older items were used for; like a standing four-legged mailbox on a street corner, a VCR player, a dial hard line phone, an old Superman type phone booth, and even a call box. I find this funny. The recruits think I'm an asshole.

- **Author's Note**: I have known Chief Eric Mason for almost 40 years now. He has been a peer, a role model, and a friend. I thank him for allowing me to continue my bi-annual rants to the recruits. He certainly is not an asshole, but he jokes that he is the head asshole in charge.

Chapter Five

He Had a Hat

"The true guide of life is to do what is right"

- Winston Churchill

I can't tell this story enough because it fits every occasion. I included it in my last book, *This is not Your Mother's Cookbook*.

On a bright sunny day, a young lifeguard took up his post on his raised white, wooden chair overlooking the water. It wasn't long before he heard the frantic cries from an elderly woman. She was standing on the edge of the sand and yelling towards the open ocean. Her grandson had been caught up in a riptide and was being swept out to sea. The boy was unfamiliar with riptide procedure, swimming parallel to the shore, and was struggling violently to get back in. He was having no success and was tiring quickly. The lifeguard sprang into action, sprinting along the beach and then diving head first into the raging surf. He surfaced clinging to his handheld rescue buoy. The riptide soon grasped him and dragged him further out directly to the now choking boy. The lifeguard focused on his target and soon closed the distance on his drowning victim. As the lifeguard drew close, the boy reached out in a panic grip that would surely drown the two of them. The lifeguard was able to fight off the boy and spin him around so that he could maintain a cross-chest rescue carry. It took a major effort as the riptide was still carrying the twosome farther out. The guard was proficient with the proper procedure and remained calm as he swam past the current and then made his way back to shore the long exhausting way around. The lifeguard finally reached the beach and carried the now lifeless figure out of the water. He bent over and initiated rescue breathing until the victim responded and spit out a mouthful of the salty water. The young man rolled over and collapsed after his super heroic efforts. As the lifeguard lie on his back catching his own breath, the little grandmother appeared over him blocking out the brilliant sun. She leaned down so her face was inches from the lifeguard's face and said to him, "He had a hat."

Sometimes it doesn't matter what you do because it is never enough. This is the motto of Law Enforcement and should replace Protect and Serve on the side of the patrol car. Like I have said, the majority of Law Enforcement Officers are truly good people that try every day to do good things, sometimes impossible things, to help total strangers. Let me start this chapter with this example. In an editorial piece in the Star Ledger[18] the writer offers a backhanded compliment, if that's what you want to call it, to the Newark Police Department. *The City of Newark reached a milestone: it's first homicide-free calendar month in 44 years* (1966)[19]. This of course is a horrendous thing to celebrate and it basically wasn't. As the time period closed marking the end of the death-free streak, the cops did not have a party but went about their business as usual. The same techniques that led to the decrease in crime would return to haunt the Department and Police as a whole a

[18]   Joan Whitlow, *"A murder-free month is worth nothing,"* The Star Ledger pg. *15* (Friday, April 2, 2010).

[19]   James Quealty & Sharon Adarlo, *"Newark sees first homicide-free month in four decades,"* The *Star Ledger* pg. 13 (April 2010).

decade later. Major crack downs, sweeps, and aggressive patrol methods would be labeled racist and an overuse of force. One great complaint of excessive force occurred when Patrol Officers observed a suspect fire two shots from a gun. They, of course, fired back wounding him. More than 70 protesters marched and called for justice. They wanted the Police to admit they were wrong.[20] This is where public opinion has gone. People believe television shows where Police can yell out the warning, "Halt Police" and the suspect throws down his weapon allowing the Police to peaceful place him under arrest. That never happens in real life. To a suspect "Halt, Police" means run like hell. The back story to this last example was the weapon had been a starter pistol with blank rounds. There is no way to determine the make, model, or caliber of a weapon, nor determine if the weapon is real, a starter pistol, or a toy from any distance if the actor is firing it, especially if the actor is firing it at you, unless of course you write for a newspaper from the cozy safety behind your desk, then you are a firearms expert. Sometimes, even after all the facts are released to the public, it remains never enough to satisfy them. There was a great outcry across the nation for all Patrol Officers to wear bodycams to show exactly what takes place when Police respond to a call. After bodycams started being worn by Officers, some groups reversed their position, stating the cameras made them look guilty. Is there any logic here? Cambridge researchers found a 93% decrease in the number of complaints made against Officers.[21] There are over 100 very expensive high-tech cameras covering the Super Bowl from every possible angle, with eight referees watching the action, and a time out for reviewing the play up close in super slow high-def action. The game takes place live before 100,000 witnesses. With all those precautions built in to make sure the game is *"fair"*, it is still difficult to determine where the little ball should be placed on the field, or if a touchdown was scored, and sometimes, they get the call wrong! The public expected the Officer's

---

[20]   Tom Hayden, *"Marchers call for justice for man shot by police"* The Star Ledger (Feb 18, 2012).
[21]   Editorial, *"Body cameras bring justice to cops, public"* The Star Ledger, (Oct. 8, 2016), N.P.

bodycams to answer all their questions. It did not and will not. Body-worn cameras have long been touted as the answer to keeping cops – and the public – honest about their interactions. Sometimes cell phones fill the void, but there are always gaps that create more questions. The cameras themselves may cost a few hundred bucks each, but the annual bill for operating these systems can run over $100,000.[22] Police responded to a call where a man beat his grandmother to death with a baseball bat. The Officers shot and killed the suspect after he advanced upon them in a threatening manner. The media pushed back on the point that no one would say how many shots were fired, how many struck the suspect, or where he was hit.[23] The answer is simply, enough, and in the correct place. Any other information is irrelevant. They missed the part where the suspect beat his grandmother to death with a baseball bat. The general public also believes in the, *High Noon* good guy/bad guy gunfight scenario that takes place on Main Street. Even the 1952 movie wasn't a fair fight. For starters it was four bad guys against one good guy and if it weren't for Gary Cooper's wife, he would have been left dead in the dirt. The media loves pointing out that the Police take advantage of the suspects by doing things like shooting back, exactly as they had been trained to do. *Two brothers who came up short in a gun battle with police...were both shot in the back. Police spokesman insisted that despite the officers identifying themselves as cops, the brothers were coming at them shooting when the police returned fire.*[24] Of course there are many factors that come into play regarding this incident like; distance, time, lighting conditions, verbal directions being shouted, position of suspects to police, and probably a hundred other things. That all doesn't matter when the headline reads, *Cops shot 2 in the back.* That is all that is needed to rile up the public. There is no need to read the article. The cops were wrong, period. The media

---

[22]   Matt Gray, "*Why police in some state's largest towns don't have bodycams*" The Star Ledger, (July 5, 2020), Pg. 1

[23]   "*Police kill man suspected of slaying grandmother,*" *The Star Ledger* (Thurs, Feb. 25, 2010).

[24]   Murray Weiss & Sean Gardiner, "*Cops shot 2 in back, Slain brothers had fired on police*", NY Post (Oct. 28, 2008)

has spoken and their judgment has been passed. These Police officers and all the others that fall into a similar category should not pass go and not collect $200. They should immediately turn in their badges, resign from the force, and report directly to jail as they were tried, convicted, and found guilty by a reporter who has absolutely no clue what real danger encompasses.

Chapter Six

The Apple

And God said, Let us make man in our image ...

- Genesis 1:26-28[25]

I have one more irreverent metaphor to give you before we get to the meat of the matter. Please excuse me but I need to continue the asshole reference a bit more. God created Adam and put him in a perfect place, which is no longer recognizable today. Adam had everything he could want and all the animals were his friends. He had all the food he could eat and everything was beautiful. All God wanted to do was sit back and observe his creation. What does Adam do? He whines to God that he was lonely. God said be careful what you wish for, but Adam wouldn't stop so God created woman. Man has been paying for that one ever since. Sorry I couldn't resist that one. Adam was the first asshole. Eve shows up and now everything is once again right with the world. God gives them ONE rule. Don't eat the fruit from the forbidden tree.

---

25   King James Version (KJV)

That later changed to an apple because it sounded better in print. ONE rule! What does Eve do? She bugs Adam to eat the fruit with her. Bam, eternal damnation. And just like that, Eve is the second asshole. Adam and Eve had two sons. Cain was the first one born and then Able came along and he was the first one to die because Cain killed him. Able must have pissed off Caine so he was the third asshole and Caine was the fourth asshole for being the first murderer. The population on Earth at that time was four. There was one law. The murder rate was then 25%. Compare that to Tijuana with 138 murders in 2018, and Tijuana only had a murder rate of .0007%. Do not vacation in the Garden of Eden. Fast forward several thousand years. We now have about eight billion assholes (Or potential assholes, giving kids the benefit of the doubt) living on earth. There are probably at least 100 rules, regulations, or laws for each individual asshole. How did they think that was going to work out since we did such a piss poor job when we only had one law? But I digress. I blame the whole Garden of Eden fiasco on the apple. Thousands of years later we have come full circle. A giant corporation called Apple has given us a bite too big for us to swallow. The iPhone, or whatever brand of cell phone you choose, is now our forbidden fruit. It could have been the answer to all our prayers but it seems to be the beginning of our demise. I know I depend upon it for shear memory. I call it my brain because I am losing mine. Humanity has taken a perfect thing and turned it against ourselves as we do with everything we touch. Sexual predators use the phone to lure victims to them. Scam artists use it to steal money from the unsuspecting. Kids use it to taunt their peers to the point of suicide. And cops… use it to lose their jobs. Remember, The Fish Story? Well now we don't have to run back to the patrol car for the Polaroid. Now it's in our back pocket and we can immediately disseminate horrible career ending photos. My Department had a NO Cell Phone rule when they first came out. Of course, the officers violated it immediately and that was before everyone was addicted to their phones. The rule went out the window one fine day when our Police radio system was knocked out and the only way, we could communicate was, you guessed it, by cell phone. Magically, cell phones appeared in all patrol cars that day and never left. What happens in The Garden of Eden, stays in The Garden of Eden, no longer holds true. EVERYTHING on your cell phone is forever. When you finally commit that one move that will land you in a jackpot, you will have a corroborating witness to verify you are an asshole. Bye-bye career, bye-bye pension, bye-bye family. Your cell phone can be subpoenaed and dumped for all its juicy information. Remember the rules of stupid:

1. Police must document their stupidity and
2. Police must share their stupidity with others, as soon as possible.

Prosecutors know these rules and will be more than happy to relieve you of your pocket buddy. Never, ever use your personal cell phone for police business. I use the following as a slide to demonstrate my point to the class:

The National Security Agency (NSA) is responsible for global monitoring, collecting, decoding, translation and analysis of information and data for counterintelligence purposes. In other words, they have collected files on everyone including pictures of your penis that you have texted to someone.

Fox News host, Greg Gutfeld, captured the thought, "Everything is being filmed, So, any public rant you do to a clerk at a shoe store, that scars you eternally."[26] Future employers now search through social media to determine if their potential candidate is an asshole, or worse. Here are a couple examples of the past coming back to bite you in the ass. This also demonstrates that cops are not the only stupids in the room. A recent outrage started in February 2020, when some Florida Democrats called for the resignation of Republican State Rep. Anthony Sabatini after a photo of him wearing blackface in high school resurfaced (of course anonymously). The photo, was taken when he was a 16-year-old sophomore.[27] The question is, who wasn't stupid in high school? That is

---

[26] Greg Gutfeld, *"MAY19, 2015"* in The Gutfeld Monologues, Classic Rants from the Five, Threshold Editions, (2018) pg. 252
[27] Michael Brice-Saddler, *"A politician wore blackface to dress as his friend. They call it a silly high school prank."* washingtonpost.com, (Feb. 7, 2019)

the period of your life to shake out most of your stupid. The lawmaker, now 30 (14 years later), explained that he and one of his good friends — a former classmate who is black — chose to dress as each other for homecoming week that year as part of a "silly high school prank." It's shocking that members of different political parties would stoop to such petty cheap shots!

And one more for the road, another identical incident took place, of course in New Jersey, when a Bergen County school board member resigned in July 2020, after a picture of him in blackface was made public. The picture was from when the board member was in high school and was surprisingly found recently on Facebook.[28] The incident had taken place over twelve years ago (when he was a stupid kid in high school). There is no escaping your past anymore no matter how long ago your indiscretion took place or how trivial it may have been for whatever reason.

I was saved from almost this very same disaster. My wife had handmade Halloween pumpkin costumes for the family. To complete the ensemble, required an orange face paint. To our horror, the substance did not wash off easy. I was saved because the next day was a Sunday and when I arrived at work, still slightly tainted orange, I was assigned inside to work the desk operations. In the poorly lit florescent room, I looked like I had just returned from vacation with a crappy tan. Thank goodness no one was offended by my orangeness. Today, I do not know if I would have fared so well.

---

[28] *"Bergen County member resigns over blackface controversy"* The Star Ledger, (July 5, 2020), Pg. A17

Chapter Seven

Damned if You Do – Damned if You Don't

"It's not how many times you get knocked down that
counts, it's how many times you get back up."

- George A. Custer

There are times when you follow all the rules in the book and
everything still goes to shit. I will provide some examples in no particular
order of importance.

I already mentioned the decrease in murders in Newark. The
reporter said, "it was worth nothing." Just a year prior to this momentous
murder-free month, the Newark Police Department reported civilian
complaints against the force had been dropping steadily – from 612 in
2006, to 578 in 2007, to 485 in 2008.[29] Do they heap praise upon this
Department for making great strides in Police/Community relations,
dropping complaints almost 80%? No, they basically accused the Police
of skullduggery. "A Police Department that investigates itself is a petri

---

[29]   Editorial, *"Draw back the curtain,"* The Star Ledger, (April 15, 2009*)*

dish for trouble." [30] The conclusion was that all would be right with the world if the local councilman would assist citizens in filling out the complaints and work with the ACLU to make sure everything was aboveboard. How could that be anything but fair?

* * *

The Camden Police Department paid out $2.25 million to families that tragically lost their children. The young kids apparently climbed into the trunk of an abandoned car in the yard of one of the kid's family. The Police did not find them. The suit alleged that the failure of the Police to follow set procedures in the search for the boys contributed to their deaths. A family member discovered them 48 hours after their disappearance.[31] These were very young children and no one had been watching them but it was the fault of the Police that they had climbed into an old car and died.

* * *

A similar incident took place in Gary, Indiana. Following a horrific high-speed traffic accident, there was a call for the Police Chief to resign. The vehicle contained four teens but only two of them were located at the crash scene. The other two were found hours later by a relative. A medical examiner determined the two had died instantaneously, after being ejected from the vehicle, of blunt force injuries that were not survivable. Of course, the grief-riddled family believed otherwise. One said "Only God knows if they were alive or not" (after the crash).[32] They disregarded the opinion of a medical professional, the alcohol involved,

---

[30] Editorial, *"Draw back the curtain,"* The Star Ledger, (April 15, 2009)

[31] "Kin of boys who died in trunk settle for $2.25M," *The Star Ledger* (April 25, 2010)

[32] Thom Patterson, *"Questions follow a son's tragic death,"* CNN.com, (Sept., 27, 2007)

and the reckless speed as contributing factors to the crash. The blame was placed squarely on the responding officers.

*   *   *

At times the police are the bad guys for not taking action. In Sioux Falls, South Dakota, the Troopers exercised their discretion, and probably common sense, by not ticketing their Boss, the Governor, for speeding. The Head of the S.D. State Police stated he never had issued orders to go easy on the Governor nor did he tell them not to stop him. Governor Bill Janklow was later elected to Congress but resigned shortly afterward when he was convicted of second-degree manslaughter after he ran a stop sign and struck and killed a motorcyclist.[33] The natural conclusion is that the Congressman would have had a stellar career and the motorcyclist would be alive today had Janklow been issued a speeding ticket at the earlier stop.

*   *   *

Acting in self-defense is no longer a good reason to take proper action. When a Mt. Olive Officer arrived at the door of a Budd Lake home, a suspect charged at him with a serrated knife. The suspect ignored the officer's commands to drop the knife and the Officer fired three shots, striking the suspect in the chest (center mass as taught – nice shooting), killing him. The suspect's father stated there was no reason to shoot his son because he was mentally ill. The suspect had already stabbed the father prior to the Police arrival.[34] Dealing with the mentally ill is never an easy task. It often ends badly and many times in suicide by cop.

*   *   *

---

[33]   Associated Press, *"S.D. cops never ticketed official whose speeding ended in death,"* The Star Ledger, (n.d.)

[34]   Star Ledger Staff, *"Lunge with knife, then fatal shots: Mt. Olive police officer kills mentally ill man who turned violent in episode at home,"* The Star Ledger (Oct., 12, 2004) pg. 15

The family will naturally take the side of a family member and will turn the situation around to put the onus on the Police, even though it was the family member that called for the Police to handle the situation that they could not.

A 16-year-old high school dropout held his 10-year-old brother at knife point. The younger boy had to jump out a second-floor window to escape. In total fear for her life the mother fled out of the house to neighbors begging for help. When Police arrived they found the suicidal, drunk youth in an uncontrollable state. The boy attacked the Officers with a butcher knife. The Officers fired at the boy sending him (alive) to the hospital. What does the mother say? "Why did they shoot? He's only 16 years old."[35] This was a serious problem, and out of control, long before the Police arrived on the scene.

*   *   *

Then there are times when something doesn't appear quite right. A homeless man who gained notoriety after being awarded a $230,000 settlement for being evicted from a Morristown library due to offensive odor and loitering, somehow remained homeless. He was again evicted from the Summit train station for loitering. He filed a $5 million lawsuit Civil Rights lawsuit against multiple agencies. My Department was later dropped from the suit.[36]

*   *   *

This is one of my favorites. A suspected shoplifter was confronted by mall security. He forcefully grabbed a random shopper away from her husband and pulled her inside a store by her hair with a knife to her throat. An off-duty Woodbridge Police Officer stepped up and went above and beyond the call of duty by taking action that led to him shooting and killing the suspect and saving the hostage's life. The

---

[35]   Judith Lucas, *"Mom: Clash over attending school led cops to shooting son,:* The Star Ledger N.d.)

[36]   Gabriel Gluck, *"Homeless activist is dropping lawsuits: Complaints targeted Summit, NJ Transit,"* The Star Ledger, (March 3, 2006) n.p.

woman and her husband were unharmed.[37] I am guessing the victim
was the same little grandmother on the beach that told the lifeguard
that the boy had a hat. She later sued the Police Department for $5
million for post-traumatic stress. She would not have had any "post"
anything were it not for the heroic efforts of the Officer. Had I or any
one of my family members been the hostage, I would still be cooking
the Officer dinner every night. It is truly a thankless job.

*   *   *

On the other end of the spectrum, here is an example when Police
were criticized for Not killing someone. A horrible domestic custody
dispute turned tragic when an off-duty Police Sergeant killed his former
wife on an Asbury Park street in the presence of their young daughter.
The Sergeant crashed into her car forcing it to stop. He then fired
eight shots into her, killing her. Fellow Officers from his Department
responded and surrounded him as he held his gun to his head. They
were able to talk him down and take him in to custody.[38] I am not
dissecting the procedure that was followed or not followed that day.
I would bet there are numerous things that should have been done,
including shooting him dead, but the victim was already dead. I can't
imagine the stress the Officers were under, facing someone who they
worked with, or for, with the possibility that they would have to kill
him. The main complaint from the public was that the Police didn't
shoot the Sergeant because he was their friend, and they also throw in
the fact that he was white, because they always have to add that to the
mix. One quote stated, "If he had not been a Police Sergeant, he would
have been shot like any other citizen." Any other citizen is usually not
shot by the Police.

*   *   *

---

[37]   Star Ledger Staff, *"Cop kills hostage-taker at mall: Knife-wielding man shot,
sparking chaos at Woodbridge Center,"*
[38]   Mary Ann Spoto & Alex Napoliello, *"Cop kills ex-wife in front of child,"* The
Star Ledger, (June 17, 2015) Pg. 1

These were just some examples where Officers walked into a situation that quickly turned into OBPOS. Many times, as in The Fish Story, the Police bring hell down upon themselves. The following are a collection of bad judgment calls, again, in no particular order.

*   *   *

Fireworks and bottle rockets seized by the County Narcotics Strike Force that were supposed to be destroyed but instead were set off, triggering a truck fire and also damage to a car. Criminal charges were not filed but Officers faced Department discipline.[39]

A follow up editorial[40] pointed out that this behavior, coupled with a previous, alcohol infused, Labor Day party (7 months prior) in another municipality where there was vandalism to property along with, yes, fireworks again[41], were examples of local cops deciding certain laws didn't apply to them. The anonymous editorialist makes a strong point that not only were the Officers entitled to violate several laws but also received more lenient treatment than the citizens they were sworn to protect.[42] The author also alleged a cover-up of the three-month investigation, writing that some information was released by the Prosecutor because he feared an eventual leak.

*   *   *

This one is terrible but all other cops would laugh at it and be thankful it wasn't them. An Officer from the Tularosa, New Mexico Motor Transportation Police Division was participating in a Career Day program when he pulled his Department-issued Taser from his holster

---

[39]   Judith Lucas, "*Detectives fireworks fiasco sparks disciplinary charges,*" The Star Ledger, (April 20, 2006) Pg. 23

[40]   Editorial, "*To serve and destroy,*" The Star Ledger, (April 27,2006) pg. 4

[41]   Jennifer Golson, "More cops linked to parking deck party," The Star Ledger, (Feb. 19, 2006) Pg. 41

[42]   Editorial, "*To serve and destroy,*" The Star Ledger, (April 27,2006) pg. 4

to display it at an elementary school, accidently shooting a 10-year-old.[43] If you read the footnote, you can see that anything can be found on-line and also lives forever. The boy had a great story to tell for the rest of his life. I'm guessing his college was probably paid for. I'm also guessing the Officer also gained a moniker from his peers that he carried to his retirement, because cops are also unforgiving in their cruelty.

*   *   *

It is a lot more fun to be collectively stupid than to be stupid all by yourself, but don't forget, I mentioned at the beginning that bosses and politicians can also happily escort you into that OBPOS. In 1996 then Governor of New Jersey, Christie Whitman* wanted to show the public she was tough on crime. She piled into one of two vans full of State Troopers to make a drug sweep in Camden. At one point the team jumped out and ordered a bunch of young black men against a wall. The middle-aged white woman then exited the van after the scene had been thoroughly secured.

The brave Governor then frisked 16-year-old, Sherron Rolax, after he had already been checked. This of course was for a publicity photo, which became known as a flagrant racist picture of the Governor smiling as she patted down a black juvenile. Like Pearl Harbor, this photo would live in infamy.[44] It is unknown what shit befell the accompanying Troopers, but they had a pretty good excuse - their boss's boss told them to do it. Rolax was shot and killed 12 years later only three blocks from the spot where he met the Governor.[45]

*   *   *

---

[43] Department of Public Safety Citizen Complaint Form, http://www.. thesmokinggun.com/doucumant/cop-taserskif-687452 (May 4, 2012)

[44] Rick Hepp & John Martin, Used by the Governor, killed by the streets – Camden man frisked by Whitman is shot dead 12 years later," The tar Ledger (May 28, 2008) Pg. 11

[45] Rick Hepp & John Martin, Used by the Governor, killed by the streets – Camden man frisked by Whitman is shot dead 12 years later," The tar Ledger (May 28, 2008) Pg. 11

- **Author's Note**: Full disclosure on my relationship with Gov. Whitman. I was accosted by her security detail as they were doing their job by keeping an unknown person from getting too close to her (Read about it in my book *Shut Up When You Talk to Me*).[46] Ironically, I later assisted with her security detail when she visited Summit to dedicate the newly renovated train station. On another occasion, I had breakfast with her (and many other people) at the Governor's Mansion known as, Drumthwacket, located at 354 Stockton St., Princeton, N.J. We later had a falling out when she borrowed a billion dollars from the Police & Fire Pension Fund but forgot to repay it. To be clear, she has no idea who I am.

There are several levels of stupid and Law Enforcement manages to check off all the boxes. A Chandler, Arizona, Maricopa County Sheriff Department, K9 Sergeant possibly forgot that he was indeed a K9 Officer. He left his partner, a 5-year old Belgian Malinois, in his patrol vehicle for 12 hours, on a 109-degree day (in fricken Arizona).[47] He basically cooked the dog to death. He was charged with animal cruelty. Normal adults do this to their children more than you can imagine. So much so that they came out with a Public Service Announcement warning parents not to kill their children. The PSA offered one helpful hint: to place something important in the back seat with your child so you don't forget to take them with you. What is more important than your child?

*   *   *

I told you New Jersey hasn't cornered the market on stupid and bad decisions. A Clayton County, Georgia Officer went a little too far with a hoax. The Officer and a friend (because sometimes you need a good buddy to be really stupid) claimed during a news conference that they had discovered Bigfoot's corpse and had it on ice. The Chief of the

[46]   Robert D'Ambola, *"Shut Up When You Talk to Me"* (USA: Xlibris, 2011), Pg. 96
[47]   "Cop charged in police dog's hot car death," CNN.com,(Set. 7, 2007)

Department was not amused but was nice enough to provide the Officer with a great deal more free time to pursue his Social Media Videos.[48] The *former* Officer said the joke had gotten out of hand. They take their Bigfoot sightings very seriously in Georgia.

*   *   *

A truly classic tale was again brought to you by the best dressed Troopers of the New Jersey State Police (NJSP). After this event, their motto should have been changed from "Honor, Duty, Fidelity" to "Go Big or Go Home". On March 30, 2012, two Troop cars escorted a caravan of at least 25 to 30 high-end performance cars such as Porches, Ferraris, and Lamborghinis, southbound on the Garden State Parkway at speeds of over 100 mph. A witness dubbed the escort, "DEATH RACE 2012!" The media loved this and ran with it. Not only was the entire caravan speeding in broad daylight, but also weaving in and out of other traffic like a NASCAR race.[49] If you have ever driven the Parkway, you already know it is worse than NASCAR. It was probably an accident, but somehow the license plates of the sports cars were taped over so you couldn't read them. How could that have happened?

I wish I were a fly on the wall of the Superintendent's office when he got that call. I'm guessing his reply was, "WTF?" Once again, I believe this was one of those occasions where a situation had gotten carried away. All Law Enforcement Officers love to drive fast. It's a perk of the job that you get to do it in someone else's car using their gas. I always said a cop funeral procession should be at least 80 mph. Now imagine you have your Police cop motor revved up and you are on the road with many other monster machines. Testosterone levels are shooting off the charts. The only thing left to do is put the pedal to the metal. After all, who is going to notice a line of high-priced sports cars with marked State Police units going 100 mph on a bright and sunny Friday afternoon?

---

48   "Bigfoot Hoaxers Say It Was a Big Joke," AOL news
49   Christopher Baxter, *"Christie, A.G. condemn 'Death Race' – Call for accountability after State Police linked to caravan,"* The Star Ledger, (April 23, 2012) Pg.1

When stupid happens or a crime is committed by Officers, there are a few basic details that must be included in every subsequent article covering the incident until the public interest finally wears out; #1. Name of officer (for total embarrassment), #2. Time on the job (this indicates if they should have known better – of course they should have known better no matter how many years of service), #3. Their current salary (to show the public how their money is being wasted).

Sgt. 1st Class (Name), a 25-year veteran of the force, earned a regular salary of about $102,000 last year, not including overtime or other pay, State records show. Trooper #2 (Name), who has been on the force for six years, earned a regular salary of about $70,000 last year.[50]

The American Automobile Association (AAA) condemned the incident. They stated that. "It was troubling when the lives of innocent people are put in jeopardy because a few law enforcement professionals view themselves as above the law."[51] The AAA doesn't just condemn anyone and they were pissed.

The Superintendent attempted to separate this behavior from the rest of the State Police, and "emphasized that unprofessional actions would not be tolerated." He pointed out that the Sergeant was a 25-year road Trooper who had saved an occupant from a burning vehicle and the signature event of his career is going to be this (OBPOS)." The two Troopers involved were suspended without pay and several station commander was reassigned for their role in the incident.[52]

A story like this is too good to let die and so it lingered for as long as the media got printable ink out of it. The good news for the Troopers was that the anger towards them soon turned against higher-ups. Governor Chris Christie, a man known to be blunt, said, "What are you going to do? It's a completely ridiculous story. Shouldn't have happened. Dumb thing to do, but let me assure you, it's not the last

---

[50]   Christopher Baxter, *"High-Speed Investigation Widens, 2 Troopers suspended in Death Race probe,"* The Star Ledger, (April 24, 2012), Pg. 1
[51]   Christopher Baxter & James Queally, *"State Police call scandal aberration,"* The Star Ledger, (April 25, 2012) Pg. 1
[52]   Ibid

dumb thing we'll see happen. People are human beings, they make mistakes, and I'm glad nobody got hurt."[53]

There was no outrage, no anger, no promise to get to the bottom of this or threats that and heads would roll. Instead the Governor **assured** the public, you haven't seen nothing yet. We can be much dumber than a simple car race. The appropriate title to this editorial was "Boys will be boys." This does not leave the most taxed public in the country a warm and fuzzy feeling inside and generates absolutely NO support for Law Enforcement. Statements like this only lead to further investigations.

Only days after the story hit the front pages, the Sergeant's attorney opened his own investigation. The lawyer stated, "The State Police have escorted dozens of similar caravans in the past, though not at high speeds."[54] The question then arose as to who had approval for these matters and how many times had this occurred? The press did their digging and uncovered the Troopers private driving records, although they could not get the driving records while on duty. Then there was the question, did the cars pay the tolls on the Parkway and Atlantic City Expressway? This shoots back to the taxpayers getting the short end. If they skipped the tolls the death penalty was certainly in order.

A person who requested anonymity because they were not allowed to discuss the matter, but had no problem discussing the matter (because there is no integrity anymore), provided the press with the names of three Troopers who had been reassigned. A total of ten commanders were transferred in light of the ongoing investigations.[55]

The State Police declined requests to release their escort policy but The Star Ledger obtained it through a source with access to the division's internal policies, who was not allowed to disclose the document (another person who should be fired for violating their job requirements). A retired former Deputy Superintendent said, "Policies are not always followed word-for-word. And superior officers often delegate their

---

[53]   Editorial, *"Boys Will Be Boys,"* The Star Ledger, (April 25,2012), Pg. 14

[54]   Christopher Baxter & James Queally, *"Lawyer: Troopers led dozens of car caravans,"* The Star Ledger,(April 26, 2012) Pg. 1

[55]   Christopher Baxter, *"Shake-up topples three top troopers,"* The tar Ledger, (April 29, 2012) Pg. 1

responsibilities to lower levels, especially on routine matters….is every little nuance followed? Well there is a human factor involved."[56]

That last comment blows the entire chain of command, as well as rules and regulations, out of the water. That is the basic foundation of Law Enforcement. If these things are not followed, the entire game plan goes to shit. And in this case, it did. The editorial of the same date as this last comment was just as blistering. It stated the State Police had a sensible policy regarding escorts that was ignored. They basically accused the Superintendent of tap-dancing around the problem. The last statement in the editorial reads as follows: "At this point, it is difficult to have confidence in the State Police's self-policing. The Legislature needs to drop its hesitation and get involved.[57]

Pardon me while I interject some personal comments. This is my rule on rules. All organizations and businesses have a set of rules to guide them along and keep them on the right track. Without these rules it is the proverbial herding chickens, scenario. No one ever knows when they cross the line into the dark realm if there is no line. As things change, the rules need to be updated to conform to present conditions. Rules that are no longer applicable need to be updated or discarded completely. Everyone in the organization must know that there are indeed, rules that govern them and their behavior, and the way they operate. Not only must they know of the existence of these rules, everyone needs to read and understand them. In many cases the employee is required to sign off that they did read and understand the rules. That is the rule. The organization really only cares that the employee signed the paper to relieve them of any liability, should that employee violate the rules. There is rarely any test to make sure the employee really does know the rules. Rules are not suggestions to be interpreted as the employee sees fit. That's why they are called rules. In the movie Star Trek IV: *The Voyage Home,* Admiral Kirk

---

[56] Christopher Baxter, "*State Police policy at odds with top cop – Internal document say using troopers as escorts requires high-level approval,*" The Star Ledger, (May 4, 2012) Pg. 1

[57] Editorial, "*Lack of Self-Policing-State Police Broke their own Rules on High-Speed Escorts,*" (The Star Ledger, (May 8, 2012) Pg. 2 Sec. 2

returns to Earth after finding Spock and collecting extinct whales. For their part in saving the planet, all charges (Conspiracy, Assault on Federation Officers, Theft of Federation Property; The Enterprise, Sabotage, Willful destruction of Federation Property; The Enterprise, and Disobeying direct orders of a Starfleet Commander) against the *Enterprise* crew are dropped, save one for disobeying a superior officer, which is solely levelled at Admiral Kirk. Kirk is demoted to the rank of Captain and returned to the command of a starship.[58] Captain Kirk totally understands this because, if it were not for the rules, then Star Fleet would not exist. There was a necessity for maintaining discipline in the Chain of Command.

Constant front page news always brings the heat, especially to politicians. After two weeks into this fiasco, the chairman of the State Democratic Party was now considering legislation to change the way escorts were authorized.[59] Apparently no one about to jump into this investigation had read the existing rules yet (and why should they), because there was already a set policy covering the matter. It was very simple to determine that the current rules were violated. They needed to start the investigation with why were they violated.

The State Police policy clearly states that escorts should be tightly controlled in the upper ranks of the force and allowed judiciously – in cases such as high-profile funerals or for top government officials.[60] I have not read the actual policy but I would bet that there is no inclusion for sports cars traveling at dangerous speeds and in a reckless manner. That doesn't matter because politics and government officials hunt flies with a sledgehammer. The simple answer is someone fucked up. The next question was who.

This OBPOS continued for at least another seven years. The Sergeant and Trooper subsequently forfeited their jobs with the State Police. The Sergeant pleaded guilty and was sentenced to one year of probation. The Trooper pleaded not guilty and was accepted into

58   Wikipedia, Star Trek IV: The Voyage Home
59   Christopher Baxter & Megan DeMarco, "*Leader of State Police called on to testify about escort protocol*," The Star Ledger, (May 10, 2012) Pg. 13
60   Ibid

a program for first-time offenders. Another Sergeant, who was not involved with Death Race 2012, was awarded $445,400, after filing a whistleblower lawsuit regarding this incident. This second Sergeant had been told to destroy a letter of commendation to the Death Race Sergeant for his handling of the escort [61] You cannot make this shit up!

Wait, we're not done beating this dead horse yet. That award was appealed and the case was thrown out. It was later heard by the State Supreme Court, seven years after the infamous escort, and they overruled the appeals court and sent it back for further judgment.[62]

If you could get one glimmering light from this entire shit show, it was that the 25-year veteran Sergeant, stepped up and took full responsibility for the incident. He also asked for leniency for the other younger Trooper involved. The Sergeant said, "I deeply regret that this matter has made an already difficult job even harder on my fellow troopers who work so diligently."[63]

*   *   *

I could fill volumes on Stupid Cop Tricks but you can find your fill for your own amusement or disgust, in any newspaper on any given day. YouTube is also another good source. I will conclude this segment with another headline grabber. This one is called *The Pooperintendent.*

"It became a part of the *morning routine* for track coaches at Holmdel High School in Holmdel, New Jersey. Show up to work, walk to the track, and spot a pile of human excrement on the ground. After a couple weeks of this disgusting routine, they reported their findings to school officials and local Police who set up a sting to bust the perpootrator." (I have to say that one was clever.) They found their suspect to be a forty two-year old man, who happened to be the Superintendent of another school district. He was arrested on May 1, 2018 at 5:45 a.m.

---

[61]   Matt Arco, "*$445,400 settlement in 'Death Race' suite – Trooper wins whistleblower case over high-speed escort,*" The Star Ledger, (July 30, 2016) Pg. 1

[62]   S.P. Sullivan, "*Death Race 2012 lawsuit revived – Whistleblower alleged cover-up in State Police case'*" The Star Ledger, (July 17, 2019) n.p.

[63]   "*N.J. State Police troopers to face criminal charges in 'Death Race 2012' case,*" NJ.com, (Posted July 27, 2017 – updated March 30, 2019)

by the Holmdel Police, and was charged with lewdness, littering, and defecating in public. He was booked, given a summons and told it wasn't that bad. He reported this incident immediately to his boss and was granted paid leave from his $147,504 a year job.[64] The Super resigned his job in July and immediately went on the attack and filed suit. Who could he possibly sue for his own repeated disgusting acts you may ask? The Police of course, because his life was ruined, because the police did their job. His attorney stated that the Police unlawfully took the Super's mug shot and maliciously distributed and disseminated it to third parties, including the media, with intent to harm his client. The attorney continued that the accusations against his client were not true. The notion that the Super was a serial pooper (Did you ever think you would hear this term?) was unfounded and frankly disgusting and unfair. This was after the person was arrested after reports of human feces had been found on the school track daily over a few weeks.[65] As sometimes is the case, the evidence of the crime (a video not the poop) was not properly processed so some of it was lost, but a pertinent section of the video was saved. The Super had been caught twice in the act and approached on a third date. The lawyer was earning his money for the defense. It was interesting that the suspect was accompanied to court by his attorney and his bodyguard.[66] Life is not fair, for good or for bad. The Super's school district agreed to pay his full salary through the end of September (Five months after his arrest), plus two month's severance pay and $23,827 in unused vacation time. The total came in over $100,000. The agreement called for nondisclosure of the terms but, you guessed it, the media obtained a copy of it through the Open Public

---

[64] Adam K. Raymond, *"Pooperintendent Found Defecating on New Jersey High School Track,"* Intelligencer, (May 4, 2018)

[65] Jeff Goldman, *"Accused 'serial pooper' resigns top job – Former school superintendent plans to file lawsuit over mug shot taken by Holmdel police'"* The Star Ledger, (July 28, 2018) pg. A3

[66] Lex Napoliello, *"Lawyers in 'pooping' case clash over video'"* The Star Ledger, (Aug. 14, 2018), n.p.

Records Act (OPRA).[67] Lo and behold, it only took five months for the Super to run out of options as the attorney fee clock ticked on. They did come up with an explanation for the pooping. They called it runner's diarrhea. "The former school Superintendent accused of defecating on a Monmouth County football field track, last spring suffered from a medical condition that affects his bowels when he runs, his attorney said."[68] The Super pled guilty to defecating in public, a noncriminal municipal offense, with a fine of $500 plus court costs. The other charges of lewdness and littering were dismissed. However, the lawsuit remained in effect against the Police. [69] The Super rationalized his disgusting actions with a litany of excuses: He had runner's diarrhea; he only pooped once and that was under the bleachers; he didn't see the portable toilets 80 feet away; if he did see them, they may have been locked, and he would not have made it the 80 feet even if he had known they were there and they were not locked.[70] I was always told if you need more than one excuse than the first one wasn't good enough. He stated that he only pooped once but school employees found excrement every day for a period of a few weeks. I'm surprised the Super didn't state that there was a copycat pooper. It never occurred to him he should run at a different time when his stomach was settled. He knew people would forgive him if it was only a one-time accident. One of the few reporters that I respect, Mark DiIonno, bought in to the, "one-time accident excuse." He wrote a nice piece saying that the coverage of the "pooperintendent", without resorting to that term, was inhumane, and basically bullying of a good person. He mentions that in stories like this about people like the Super, the subjects become pinatas for the press and the public to wack at until they break open. He ended his article with, "What we may not know is what happens to

---

[67]   Steve Strunsky, *"District to pay over $100K to ex-superintendent;"* The Star Ledger, (Aug. 15, 2018), Pg. A17

[68]   Alex Napoliello, *"Ex-schools chief pleads guilty to defecating on school grounds,"* The Star Ledger, (Oct. 25, 2012), Pg. A21

[69]   Ibid.

[70]   Ibid.

people...when we lose sight of their humanity- and ours."[71] The press has no problem doing this to Law Enforcement on a regular basis. It is no longer unbiased journalism because it has become a blood sport. The misunderstood Super continued his lawsuit claiming Holmdel Police Department's actions were the height of willful misconduct, professional irresponsibility, and a total disdain for the law.[72] That describes someone that would take a dump on a school track on a daily basis. After the mug shot was taken it appeared on the Police Department's Facebook page in May 2018 (I do not know how many likes it got). The lawsuit was contingent upon whether or not releasing such a photo was within the law or not. In September of 2019, U.S. District Court Judge Ann E. Thompson granted the motion to dismiss the lawsuit. The Judge stated that disclosure of his mug shot did not "reveal any information that was not already public" and that its purpose was to serve as a "visual of someone with pending charges."[73] The attorney warned that, "A new complaint is forthcoming in state court." Of course, there will be another lawsuit, why not? To wrap this literal OBPOS up, let me add to the comment I made regarding the press attacking Law Enforcement on a daily basis. Remember I explained about assholes? Well an Officer may be a great person, a model citizen, a pillar of the community, and an amazing dedicated Officer. That doesn't matter if the Officer is Adam and he has an asshole kid like Cain. If your kid does anything wrong, they will put YOUR name in the newspaper because you are, or were, in law enforcement. Case in point: Before they tore down the old Yankee Stadium, twenty fans were arrested collecting souvenirs like third base. The only one singled out and publicly named was the son of a retired New Jersey Police Chief.[74] That's how the press plays their

[71]   Mark DiIonno, *"Behind a punchline, a man's ruined reputation,"* The Star Ledger, (Oct. 30, 2018), Pg. 1

[72]   Joe Atmonavage, *"Ex-superintendent seeks probe by police,"* The Star Ledger, (Feb. 27, 2019), n.p.

[73]   Chris Sheldon, *"Ex-N.J. superintendent's mug shot lawsuit dismissed,"* The Star Ledger, (Oct. 8, 2019), n.p.

[74]   Denise Buffa & Erin Calabrese, *"Caught stealing at the Stadium,"* New York Post, (Sept. 23, 2008), Pg. 28

game. Public humiliation of a retired Chief is fair to them. You can't find a better cop than NYPD Commissioner Ray Kelly.[75] * His son was a TV host and also, unfortunately, an alleged asshole. The son found himself accused of sexual assault (Innocent until proven guilty unless the press says your guilty) but the headline had to drag dad into the picture, of course. It read – *In case of NYPD boss's son, savvy lawyer keeps quiet.*[76] It also criticized them for hiring a good attorney. Did you ever hear of the dentist's son being arrested, or the banker, or the doctor, or better yet, the son of a reporter? No!

* **Author's Note** – I had the honor to not only meet Commissioner Kelly but also have a brief conversation. It was some time around 2007 after an APPLE meeting. This was a public/private partnership with the NYPD and numerous corporate security teams to keep abreast of current trends in crime and terrorism (after 9/11). The Commissioner was standing alone after the meeting so I approached him and started to chat. He was very kind and accommodating. I finally asked him to sign my business card. He took my card without hesitation and signed it. He handed it back and warned me with a smile, "I don't want to see this on eBay."

• And now an obscure reference for the sports fans:

---

[75] Wikipedia -**Raymond Walter Kelly** (born September 4, 1941) was the longest serving Commissioner in the history of the New York City Police Department (NYPD) and the first man to hold the post for two non-consecutive tenures. According to its website, Kelly — a lifelong New Yorker—had spent 47 years in the NYPD, serving in 25 different commands and as Police Commissioner from 1992 to 1994 and again from 2002 until 2013. Kelly was the first man to rise from Police Cadet to Police Commissioner, holding all of the department's ranks, except for Three-Star Bureau Chief, Chief of Department and Deputy Commissioner, having been promoted directly from Two-Star Chief to First Deputy Commissioner in 1990. After his handling of the World Trade Center bombing in 1993, he was mentioned for the first time as a possible candidate for FBI Director. After Kelly turned down the position, Louis Freeh was appointed.
[76] Jennifer Peltz, *"In case of NYPD boss's son, savvy lawyer keeps quiet"* Associated Press, (Jan 29, 2012), n.p.

Tyrus (Ty) Raymond Cobb (December 18, 1886 to July 17, 1961), nicknamed The Georgia Peach, was an American Major League Baseball (MLB) outfielder. He was born in rural Narrows, Georgia. Cobb spent 22 seasons with the Detroit Tigers, the last six as the team's player-manager, and finished his career with the Philadelphia Athletics. In 1936 Cobb received the most votes of any player on the inaugural Baseball Hall of Fame ballot, receiving 222 out of a possible 226 votes (98.2%); no other player received a higher percentage of votes until Tom Seaver, in 1992. In 1999, editors at the *Sporting News* ranked Ty Cobb third on their list of "Baseball's 100 Greatest Players". Cobb is widely credited with setting 90 MLB records during his career. His combined total of 4,065 runs scored and runs batted in (after adjusting for home runs) is still the highest ever produced by any major league player. He still holds several records as of the end of the 2019 season, **including the highest career batting average (.366 or .367, depending on source)** and most career batting titles.[77]

The point of that short story was the fact that the baseball player with the best batting average of all time only hit .367. That means he only got on base slightly more than one third of the time, and this is considered an amazing feat to accomplish. Law Enforcement Officers need to hit 1.00 every day or could wind up dead or in jail.

After 9/11, the common saying was, terrorists only have to get it right once, law enforcement has to get it right all of the time! Police do not get paid to lose. Police are not supposed to retreat. Police are supposed to press forward and win every battle and make the arrest. This is a great deal of pressure placed upon a mere mortal being. You cannot lose, ever! I hope this puts the concept of One Big Pile of Shit in better perspective. This does not excuse those that do dumb or do illegal shit. That's up next.

[77] Wikipedia

Chapter Eight

Sometimes Good Guys wear Black Hats

"Hi Ho Silver"

-The Lone Ranger

The old unwritten rule of classical western films was good guys wore white hats; bad guys wore black hats. There were numerous reasons for this wardrobe decision but here is maybe the best one. If there are twenty people in the street fighting, 5 good guys, and the rest dirty rotten scoundrels, dressing them in dark and bright colors would help the audience know whether the good guys are winning.[78] Nowadays, you sometimes can't tell the players without a program.

The Lone Ranger was the best example of the white hat. He was the epitome of the all-around good guy image. He was also an enigma because he confused people by wearing a mask. As he rode off into the sunset, the people he left behind after helping them with their problems always asked,

---

[78]   Wolfhatproductions, "*Why Bad Guys Wear Black Hats*" The Film Psychologist, (Nov. 14, 2014) filmpsychologyblog.worldpres.com

"Who was that masked man?" The man who played The Lone Ranger, Clayton Moore, also lived up to his onscreen image. Today there are from 600,000 to 700,000 active law enforcement officers working across the United States. The problem is that the media takes great pleasure in highlighting the very few rotten scumbags who ruin it for all the rest.

We have already covered what Captain Kirk referred to as the "Kobayashi Maru."[79] There are unwinnable situations. Bad decisions and stupidity often plays a role in the Officer's downward spiral. Now let's take that stupidity and increase the magnitude, like cranking up the Richter scale[80] to measure the big earthquake about to hit, or as we lovingly call OBPOS. Extreme stupidity often leads directly to criminal activity. It is inconceivable that a person would work particularly hard to obtain a position in any field, not just law enforcement, only to piss it away for what they believe is a better deal. The fact that they would ever get caught does not cross their mind, or they just think they are that good that they cannot be caught. According to the Bureau of Justice Statistics, the United States has the highest incarceration rate in the world at over 2 million prisoners. They all 2 million believed they were too good to get caught. They were mistaken.

I have personally known Officers who have crossed the line and decided to play for Dr. Evil's team or have read about their misdeeds after the fact. Let me tell you, there is no shortage of stupid. Some of the favorite crimes involve vice, because of the old fairy tale, that they are "victimless" crimes. Truth be told, if there is a crime, somewhere there is a victim. These crimes include gambling, a lot of sex offenses – including running prostitution, and extortion. Then we have embezzlement, or stealing from your friends and co-workers. In 2003 the head of the

---

[79] Wikipedia - The Kobayashi Maru is a training exercise in the fictional Star Trek universe designed to test the character of Starfleet Academy cadets in a no-win scenario. The Kobayashi Maru test was first depicted in the opening scene of the film Star Trek II: The Wrath of Khan and also appears in the 2009 film Star Trek.

[80] www.britannica.com - The Richter scale was originally devised to measure the magnitude of earthquakes of moderate size (that is, magnitude 3 to magnitude 7) by assigning a number that would allow the size of one earthquake to be compared with another.

New Jersey Police Benevolent Association (NJPBA) was charged with diverting (that's a nice term for stealing) over $1 million from the Union he represented, from the people that not only elected him to office but also trusted him to watch out for them.

Cops love to arrest drunk drivers and several like to be them. This always places the arresting Officer in a bad situation that could go wrong for both of them if the proper procedure is not followed. The list continues with cheating on Police exams, tampering with official records (always a favorite), falsifying time sheets, insurance fraud, money laundering, and the catch all – official misconduct.

*   *   *

Drugs have a way of corrupting many individuals. People see it as an easy score because there is SO much cash! Who would miss it and who is going to tell on you, the bad guys? I have known Officers (after they were arrested) who took drugs and sold drugs. I never saw those incidents coming. One recruit was reported to me, when I was a supervisor, as acting strange. I passed on the information to higher ups and he was found to be under the influence while he was in the Police Academy. Needless to say, he didn't see graduation day. Is this someone you want backing you up on a call?

*   *   *

I briefly worked for a Sergeant while on special assignment with the ATTF. He was the nicest guy and was affectionately called Radar, after the MASH character. He even resembled Radar O'Reilly. After I returned to my Department, I learned that good old Radar had been arrested for bank robbery. He had subsequently been promoted to Lieutenant and had chosen a bank in the same county where he worked. When investigators reviewed the security camera footage, one said, "Boy that really looks like…", because it was. He was then investigated in connection with four other bank robberies.[81] This was a guy who started

---

[81]   Katie Wang, *"Sheriff baffled by change in ex-officer"* NJ.com (Jan. 28, 2005), n.p.

down the right path and somewhere along the way had a total mental breakdown in his personal life.

*   *   *

There are some others like Radar, that graduate directly to the big time with child porn, manslaughter, and outright murder. I was attending a course to become a firearms instructor and had a Sergeant from another Department assisting with the class. Part of the course was to get gassed to understand the effects it may have on you. The instructors also enjoyed torturing us. At the end of the day we had had enough and were crying like babies. This particular Sergeant was walking behind us with yet one more gas grenade. I politely explained to him that if he dropped it, that would be the last thing that he did. I had no idea this nut job was capable of a double homicide. I later learned that he was arrested for poisoning his wife. He was caught because at the autopsy, the Medical Examiner recalled a similar case. The wonderful sergeant had previously poisoned his mother-in-law the same way. He got away with the first murder but he doubled down on his luck because he thought he was a master criminal.

*   *   *

Another Officer made his first mistake by hanging with members of the Hell's Angels Motorcycle Gang. If you are in any way associated with law enforcement, then absolutely no good will come of this friendship. He and his two of leather-clad buddies strolled into a bar and surprisingly the Angels got into a fight. Who saw that coming? After a two-month investigation the 24-year veteran Officer was charged with official misconduct, hindering prosecution, and failing to perform his duty as a public servant. He took a plea agreement and resigned from the force. He received two years of probation and forfeited his annual pension of $61,700.[82] This last penalty could have added up to millions depending upon his life span. You can read into this story that his

---

[82]   Joe, Moszczynski, *"Off-duty cop charged with lying to police over biker gang"* The Star Ledger,)March 27 2012), pg. 1

Department was totally pissed at him for making them all look like asses. He may have been able to salvage something out of his career if he hadn't sided with the bikers.

*   *   *

I have to mention a few more stupid/criminal acts to make you feel good about yourself. When Police attend a class on drunk driving, they would have one class member drink to the point of intoxication to show the effect of alcohol on a person. They always took the precaution to make sure the person had a ride home from the class.

On one occasion, an Officer attained an alcohol reading of .13 (now .08 is considered intoxicated). He was driven home by a classmate and then proceeded to jump on his ATV, crashed, and received severe facial injuries. He was charged with Driving While Intoxicated (DWI) and other motor vehicle violations.[83] He totally missed the entire point of the class that he had just completed.

*   *   *

An Irvington Police Officer whose job it was to stop document fraud was charged with using a friend's birth certificate to obtain a New Jersey driver's license with her photo on it.[84] This is so stupid I have no comment.

*   *   *

A Sergeant was overseeing other Officers assigned to a Miley Cyrus concert. Officers assigned to the detail seized eight tickets from a scalper and turned them over to the Sergeant in charge. He then gave two tickets to a friend and failed to log the other six into evidence. I have nothing against Miley Cyrus and think she has a wonderful voice. The Cyrus Wrecking

---

[83]   Shawn Boburg, *"Cop gets DUI after class on drunken driving"* The Star Ledger, (Dec. 17, 2011) n.p.

[84]   Star Ledger Staff, Anti-fraud police officer faces charges on friend's ID" The Star Ledger, (May 1, 2008), n.p.

Ball struck the Sergeant square in the gut. The ex-Sergeant was charged with official misconduct and evidence tampering. He resigned from the Department, received Pre-Trial Intervention (PTI), probation, and paid $175 fine. He did not admit guilt in the matter. He will eventually get the charges expunged. He had once received the Department's highest award – the Medal of Valor after a furious shootout. He was known to be a brave and dedicated Police Officer. The scalper went free.[85] Miley Cyrus went on to be ranked 62nd on *Billboard's* Top 125 Artists of All-Time list in 2019.

*   *   *

The all-time winner and headline grabber was an Officer who was in the process of making a plan. Let me just leave you with the headline: *NYC cop accused of plotting to cook and eat 100 women.*[86] What kind of message does that send regarding the screening process and the way candidates are selected? Do they ask about hobbies?

*   *   *

I have said before, misery loves company. Headline - Mayor orders outside probe of Department plagued by charges against dozens of cops. In 2012, at least 23 Memphis Officers and civilian personnel were charged with crimes from DUI and drug dealing to human sex trafficking. Dozens of Officers from the 2400-Officer force have been charged with crimes over the past eight years.[87]

*   *   *

I have collected numerous stories over the years on a variety of stupid/criminal activity. Here are some headlines:

---

[85]   Ames Queally, *"Newark cop resigns after probe into missing Miley Cyrus concert tickets"* The Star Ledger, (Jan 22, 2011), pg. 1

[86]   Greg B. Smith & Rocco Parascandola, *"NYC cop accused of plotting to cook and eat 100 women"* The Star Ledger, (Oct. 28, 2012), n.p.

[87]   Drian Sainz, *"Memphis singing the blues over its police force"* The Star Ledger, (Oct. 10, 2012). n.p.

- 3 Officers suspended after leaving teens in police van overnight
- Cop admits he shot self and lied on report
- Sergeant faces charge of sexual contact on job
- Cop charged with exposing himself
- Officer accused of luring girl, 12
- Three more lose jobs in Police exam scandal
- Police chief retires amid charges of discrimination
- Cop faces DWI charge as teen run over
- Shoplifting charge brings probation for lawman
- Officer admits $16G theft from PBA
- Policeman is charged in torching his car
- Trooper convicted on 8 charges – skimming cocaine, reselling it
- Partner turns on accused 'Rape Cop'
- FBI agent accused of tipping off informant
- Texas police shake down drivers
- Drug Cop Scandal
- Cops plead guilty to gambling, lose jobs
- Ex-cop executed for Houston woman's murder
- Five cops arrested for bribery
- Finest Hitmen - Ex-NYPD detectives murdered for the mob
- Officer, wife face more charges – money laundering
- Judge gives ex-Bronx cop 7 ½ years for choking man to death
- Sex club scandal linked to many more cops
- Officer in Louima assault case is accused of perjury
- Cheating ex-cop shot in his car – by NYPD jilted wife
- Officer in kidnap enters guilty plea
- Detective admits role in auto insurance rip-offs
- NYPD's Capt. Peepers (Daily News of course)

And those were just the some of the good ones. I have one more story that I would like to mention. In 1998 I was attending a 12-week course – Police Staff & Command, at the State Police training academy in Sea Girt. Half the class was made up of State Troopers and the other half were municipal Officers. It turned out that one Officer worked for the Trenton, NJ Police Department. During the class, another Trenton

Officer, Christopher Kerins, decided to put his time to good use while attending a Police Conference in Cincinnati, Ohio, by robbing a bank and using his unmarked police car as the getaway car. It sounded like a plan at the time. He was arrested after a high-speed chase and subsequent shoot out with the good guy Police.[88]

Of course, cops are cruel and unforgiving so after we learned of this robbery, we all wore masks the next day for our fellow classmate. This was not a surprise that cops could rob banks as I have already stated. The shock of this story was that this Officer decided to wear the black hat of the bad guy after a breakdown. Nine years earlier, Kerins shot and killed an escaped mental patient who had attacked a group of Officers with a butcher knife.[89]

Kerins had been a model Officer, working undercover and serving as a K-9 Officer. The guy was a regular family man and coached his son's baseball team. A psychologist, who had studied the impact of stress on Police Officers said, "I had never encountered a case as extreme as Kerins, however, stress brought on by Police work can amount to slow victimization, spilling into other aspects of their lives."[90]

Kerins confessed to the Ohio bank robbery and also to seven others in the Trenton area where he was wanted as the "Camouflage Bandit." Apparently, he had turned to drugs after the 1989 shooting which further impacted his mental state. When he was arrested he claimed to have no actual recollection of his crimes, suffering from post-traumatic stress disorder. His son said, "I won't believe it until he tells me he did it, and then I still won't believe it." You can understand a family member saying that but his own Department refused to take the call from the Cincinnati PD because they thought it was a hoax until they verified the caller.[91] Cops see unbelievable things everyday but couldn't comprehend that a decorated hero Officer, friend, family man, could

---

[88]   Robert Rudolph, *"Double life: Cop and robber"* The Star Ledger, (Dec. 2, 1998), Pg. 73

[89]   Ibid

[90]   Ibid

[91]   bid

fall so far. What I can't believe is that NO one saw this drastic change in him over a nine-year period. No one saw that he needed help.

The article had everything – a picture of him on the high school football team, his high school graduation picture, a picture of him as a rookie Officer, and the required crazy-face picture of him as they stuffed him into a police car in handcuffs wearing the fashionable orange jumpsuit.

Kernis was sentenced to 10 years for the eight-bank robbery spree. He had nearly completed his probation, when in August 2010 he robbed his ninth bank in Hopewell, N.J.[92] This is almost as tragic as you can get.

When an Officer experiences a FUBAR (Fucked Up Beyond Any Repair) moment, there are usually several options. Number one is to resign from the job or, as they like to say in the press release, allowed to retire. This usually accompanies: and not allowed to hold a public office again. Many times, if the offense is not too serious, like driving like a maniac down the Garden State Parkway, the offender receives PTI or pre-trial intervention. This keeps them out of the criminal justice system of incarceration, contingent on the requirement that they do not follow up with a second stupid offense. The PTI was their bite of the apple, a slap on the wrist for being naughty. No Officer wants to go to jail as they are not welcome among the people who hate them. The big hit is the revocation of their pension, especially if the offender is a veteran Officer with many years paid into the system. They would get out what they put into the pension themselves, but this is no consolation when you lose the lottery ticket for a million plus dollars. And all too often the Officer goes to jail.

---

[92] *"Convicted bank-robbing NJ cop back in jail"* 6ABC Action News, WPVI-TV Philadelphia, PA

Chapter Nine

This Frog is Not a Prince

"Corruption of the best is the worst"[93]

-Jed Bartlet

When I delivered this story regarding *The Boiling Frog Syndrome* for the veteran cops of the in-service class, some of them actually booed me. I wasn't a big fan of the metaphor for a while until I came across more and more examples of real-life frogs. Here's how the story goes:

Put a frog in a pot full of water and start heating the water. As the water temperature increases, the frog adjusts its body temperature as a result. The frog maintains itself by adjusting its body temperature along with the increase in the water temperature.

Just when the water is about to reach its boiling point the frog can no longer adjust itself. At this point the frog decides to jump out. It tries to jump, but it is incapable of doing so as it has used up all its strength adjusting its body temperature. Very soon the frog dies. What killed the

---

[93] Corruptio optimi pessima, old Latin maxim

frog was his own inability to determine when the situation was getting too dangerous and his own inability to get out of the situation before it got out of control.[94]

The perfect example of the boiling frog started before I entered law enforcement in 1977. NYPD was a cesspool of corruption. The Commission to Investigate Alleged Police Corruption (which became known informally as the Knapp Commission, after its chairman Whitman Knapp), was a five-member panel initially formed in April 1970 by Mayor John V. Lindsay to investigate corruption within the New York City Police Department. The creation of the commission was largely a result of the publicity generated by the public revelations of police corruption made by Patrolman Frank Serpico and Sergeant David Durk. The Commission confirmed the existence of widespread corruption and made a number of recommendations.[95]

In the 1973 movie, Al Pacino depicted Serpico as the hopeless frog. He, unlike the frog in the story, immediately detected a dangerous change in the temperature of the Department. He wanted no part of the corruption, kickbacks, pay offs, and brutality. He attempted to jump out of the pot on numerous occasions but the system would not allow him to do so. His career ended when he was set up during a drug raid and shot in the face, allegedly, by a fellow Officer.

I mentioned in the last chapter that 23 officers on the Memphis Department had been charged with crimes over an eight-year period. This sounds like a lot (which it is), but this only represented 1% of the entire Department.

Comedian Chris Rock said it best, *"Whenever the cops gun down an innocent black man... they always say the same thing.... "It's not most cops. It's just a few bad apples." Bad apple? That almost sounds nice. I've had a bad apple. It was tart. But it didn't choke me out. Here's the thing. I know it's hard being a cop. I know it's hard. I know that shit's dangerous. I know it is, ok? But some jobs can't have bad apples. Some jobs, everybody*

---

[94] "Let's Talk About Boiling Frog Syndrome" exporingyourmind.com, (Jan. 22, 2017)
[95] Wikipedia, *"Knapp Commission"*

gotta be good. Like... pilots. You know? American Airlines can't be like, "Most of our pilots like to land. We just got a few bad apples... that like to crash into mountains. Please bear with us."

Some jobs can't have bad apples – everybody gotta be good! That should be painted on the inside wall of every law enforcement agency in the country. The family singing group the Osmonds[96] sang, *One bad apple don't spoil the whole bunch, girl.* Maybe not but it makes the rest of the apples look like shit.

Zero tolerance! I understand that people are not robots and everyone fucks up at some point, but crime is not a mistake, it's a choice. A bad one! When you take the job, you signed up to wear a white hat, end of story. I told my recruits that they may decide at some point they didn't want to do this job any more. That is perfectly alright. There are many people who cannot do a lot of jobs for 25 years, nonetheless law enforcement. Then stop doing it. Go do something else because if you start doing a bad job, it reflects on the other 600,000 that are doing a good job.

When a person voluntarily accepts a position of public trust, he takes on new obligations. If he does not want to live up to these obligations, he or she is free to decline or leave the job. Not only is this a fair demand but granting authority without expecting public servants to live up to it would be unfair to everyone they are expected to serve.[97]

When you get close to retirement, you are pretty much done, physically as well as mentally, and deserve to look forward to a new life. It would aggravate me when young Officers would start the countdown clock at 10-years in. I would tell them, "Why wait, go now, save yourself and everyone else the trouble." You cannot coast for 15 years.

Before I start the next segment, I want to repeat that every Department has their own day in the news cycle. It is only a matter of time. Reminder: all parties are innocent until proven guilty in a Court of law. I am disclosing only public information and I am not passing

---

[96] The song One Bad Apple by "The Osmonds" was released in 1971/1972 and reached number 1 in the U.S and Canada

[97] The Center for American and International Law

judgment. I am using these examples as a teaching tool. Full disclosure, my own Department became the star of a major political shit storm that made national news and set new Court precedent.

* * *

On February 9, 1984, detectives armed with a search warrant, issued by the Municipal Judge, entered the Summit Middle School and seized hundreds of student disciplinary files. The County Prosecutor called the action unconstitutional. A Superior Court Judge immediately ordered the records sealed and turned over to the Court. This made the news as far away as Hawaii.[98] (I know this because one of our Officers was on vacation and saw it in the newspaper.)

The seizure of records, with a warrant, was based on what was believed to be credible information that the school was not reporting drug and alcohol abuse by students to the police.

The Union County Prosecutor's Office started an investigation and requested a Grand Jury. The Star Ledger of course, ran a cartoon and accompanying editorial comparing us to the Gestapo (because the Nazi's were concerned about kids using drugs in school). *"It was an incident that dredged up dismaying memories of excesses in totalitarian regimes that existed in Nazi Germany and Fascist Italy – and still exists in the Soviet Union and other dictatorships. It never could happen here, a nation that prides itself on a redoubtable constitution heritage of human rights."*[99]

The PTA/PTO hired an ACLU attorney, the school board called its attorney, the Mayor called his attorney, the Police Chief called his attorney, and the City attorney was also kept very busy. The attorneys were happy. Of course, the parents were upset because they really had no idea what was going on but knew it could not possibly involve their child. At one contentious meeting, one of the, 100-watt light bulbs, stated, "When my three-year-old turns five, will he be busted for

[98]   Cindy Currence, *"Police Seizure of Student Discipline Records Provokes Outcry,"* Education Week, (Feb. 23, 1984)
[99]   The Star Ledger, Editorial, (March 1984)

scribbling crayons on the wall?" Reason always wins out in the public forum.

The Mayor blamed the School Superintendent and the Principal of the Middle School. The County Prosecutor blamed the Municipal Judge for issuing the warrant without enough probable cause. The Police blamed the Principal for covering up the problem. The Police attorney blamed the Board of Education for giving up the files. The Prosecutor's office said that the drug problem was not the concern of the Grand Jury (Why would that come into play?). A State Senator blamed the N.J. Commissioner of Education for failing to require school administrators to report illegal acts in schools. The President of the City Council blamed the Star Ledger for saying the word Gestapo.

A Superior Court Assignment Judge found the Police Department's actions violated the Fourth Amendment to the U.S. Constitution protecting citizens against unlawful seizure.[100] The people who were under investigation became known as "The Summit Seven." I have a bumper sticker that reads **"Free the Summit Seven"** as if they were a radical underground terrorist group from the 60's. Two weeks into this OBPOS, the Chief of Police stated he ordered the action and took full responsibility. This was a rare incident, even for Police screw ups, where this was truly a circle jerk effort from the top down.

The Mayor did not run for reelection, the Principal and the Chief retired, and the incident made case law. After a three-month long investigation involving over 60 witnesses, the Grand Jury (and I summarize) declared this to be One Big Pile of Shit on everyone's part.

WHEREAS, in 1985, following upon the recommendations contained in a presentment issued by a special county grand jury, the Attorney General and the County Prosecutors' Association of New Jersey issued a joint policy statement requiring that all applications for search warrants be reviewed by the Attorney General or his designees, or the

---

[100] Gabriel Gluck, *"Summit board accused of 'goof' in file seizure"* The Star Ledger, (March 27, 1984), pg.11

appropriate County Prosecutor, or his designees, prior to submission to a court for authorization...[101]

Not long after this case was put to rest, the City hired a consulting firm, for more money than it should have paid out, to do a review of the Police Department, to find out things that everyone knew, and make recommendations that were already suggested. That's how the consulting business works.

When it was my turn to sit before the panel of "experts" they asked me two or three questions and thanked me for coming in. I told them I wasn't done. They were indignantly surprised, closed their notebooks, sat back in their chairs, folded their arms in silent protest, and said, "Go ahead." They weren't getting paid to go off script to dig down into the real issues at hand. I spoke for another 30 minutes, and they never wrote down a word I said. I felt Like Arlo Guthrie sitting on the Group W Bench telling my story about Alice's Restaurant in four-part harmony. They didn't care what I had to say and they didn't like my kind. This has been a trend throughout my career.

At least I felt better getting it off my chest. After all that was said and done, a hell of a lot more was said, than done. Law Enforcement hates change. Several Officers left my Department and joined other Departments only to discover that it was the same circus with different clowns.

*   *   *

Let us turn to the Edison, New Jersey Police Department. Edison is a township in Middlesex County, New Jersey, United States, in the New York City metropolitan area. Situated in north-central New Jersey, Edison lies within the core of the Raritan Valley region. As of the 2010 United States Census, Edison had a total population of 99,967

[101] ATTORNEY GENERAL LAW ENFORCEMENT DIRECTIVE No. 2002-2 APPROVAL OF SEARCH WARRANT APPLICATIONS, EXECUTION OF SEARCH WARRANTS, AND PROCEDURES TO COORDINATE INVESTIGATIVE ACTIVITIES CONDUCTED BY MULTIPLE LAW ENFORCEMENT AGENCIES, (Aug. 8, 2002)

retaining its position as the fifth most populous municipality in New Jersey[102] The Police Department consists of approximately 180 officers. Edison came to my attention while I was perusing the newspaper for articles for my class. Edison seemed to be always in the paper. These were only some of the headlines from articles that I was able to collect. There were more. In all fairness some articles are a continuing story on specific Officers.

10.21.09	Shoplifting charge brings probation for Edison lawman
12.09.12	A Police Department's March to Self-Destruction (front page two-part special report)
10.26.13	Seven Edison cops sue over 'wagon wheel of death" (pg.1)
04.01.14	New criminal charges plague Edison police (pg.1)
04.04.14	Edison's spreading cancer – Latest charge against an officer shows his troubling reach (Editorial)
07.03.15	No room in Edison for a racist cop out on the street (editorial)
09.17.16	4 Officers admit plot for revenge
12.20.16	Ex-cop's travel limits lifted in arson case – former Officer accused of firebombing
01.03.17	In Edison, what's another scandal? (Editorial)
01.04.17	Two ex-Edison cops avoid probation in revenge plot
01.15.17	Town paid $175K to lawyers in 'lingerie cop' legal battle
08.22.17	Ex-Edison cop admits firebombing his boss
09.08.17	Ex-cop gets 20 years for firebombing home
09.20.17	Former cop avoids jail time for arson plot against Officer
12.13.17	Three cops with past arrests are promoted
01.19.18	Ex-officer sues to get job back – Lingerie cop claims he was forced out
03.21.18	Cop charged in tire slashing stripped of badge
03.23.18	Cop accused of vandalizing vehicle of ex

---

[102] Wikipedia

04.18.18	Officer charged with using Police database to stalk ex-girlfriend
05.22.18	Officers accused of using steroids
06.0218	Cops face charges in no-show jobs case – 5 Officers made more than $840,000, records show
06.08.18	More Police likely to face arrest – Prosecutor blasts system that let cops pad their pay in alleged no-show jobs
06.14.18	Taxpayers on hook for pension of lingerie cop
08.29.18	Embattled cops brace for more arrests Five have been charged, but as many as 20 could be implicated, sources say
09.29.18	Cop indicted on official misconduct charges
10.20.18	5 cops indicted over alleged no-show jobs
12.28.18	Edison Police Officer from Scotch Plains charged with tampering, obstruction
04.26.19	Jury indicts Edison cop in evidence-tampering case
09.27.19	Cop charged with hindering crash probe

My only comment is holy shit. This was an entire *army* of frogs (Army is the correct terminology for a bunch of frogs) who not only thrived in the boiling water, they reached out of the pot to grab the knob on the stove to turn up the flame. My favorite was the "Wagon Wheel of Death". This was explained by The Star Ledger (that had absolutely no love for this department except to sell a lot of papers).

Edison Police Officers refer to "the wagon wheel of death" as a hit list. On a single sheet of paper, discovered in the Internal Affairs unit, an investigator had drawn a series of circles with names inside. Two circles stood in the center, with lines like spokes of a wagon wheel, leading to other circled names. Nearly all of the Officers were outspoken supporters of the Mayor, and some were equally outspoken of the Chief... Officers contend the document shows internal affairs was used to target the Mayor's supporters.[103]

---

[103] Mark Muller, "*Seven Edison cops sue over wagon wheel of death*" The Star Ledger, (Oct. 26, 2013) pg. 7

You can see by the dates that this behavior ran over the course of a decade. At some point you would think the Officers would catch on that this was unacceptable as they watched their own comrades get suspended, arrested, go to Court, get fired and sometimes go to jail. They apparently were very comfortable with the temperature of their environment and were not bothered in the least as it became much hotter. Edison had a similar number of Officer-involved issues as Memphis but Memphis had 2400 members compared to Edison's 180. Edison's problems involved over 10% of the force.

This degree of violations commands a response, usually a take-over by the county Prosecutor's office or State Attorney General's Office or, some other oversight by another agency or monitor.

*　　*　　*

The New Jersey State Police had a history of heating the water to a boil on several occasions. (Go back and read about Death Race 2000) One issue of concern was racial profiling. Stories popped up from time to time and the State Police stated there was no such thing as profiling. I thought to myself, gee that's funny I attended a class based on profiling. The instructor didn't tell us to pull over minorities. No, they demonstrated tell-tale signs of drug trafficking, like the rear end of a car hanging lower that would indicate a heavy load. The same reason a ship travels lower in the water when it is full. They never mentioned race. Criminal activity often follows a pattern of prior suspicious behavior. This was the entire premise behind *Terry v. Ohio, 392 U.S. 1 (1968).*

Terry v. Ohio was a landmark decision of the Supreme Court of the United States in which the Court ruled that the Fourth Amendment's prohibition on unreasonable searches and seizures is not violated when a police officer stops a suspect on the street and frisks him or her without probable cause to arrest, if the police officer has a *reasonable suspicion* that the person has committed, is committing, or is about to commit a crime and has a reasonable belief that the person "may be armed and presently dangerous."[104]

This was a stop and frisk case but fully applies to profiling based upon suspicious behavior. The case does not mention race as a factor. Police instincts should not be ignored just as stopping someone based upon the color of their skin should never be allowed. Common sense should be weighed in all situations.

The Wyckoff Police Chief became embroiled in a battle with the ACLU in 2016, when they accused him of ordering racial profiling. The chief had allegedly sent an email stating, "Profiling, racial or otherwise, has it's (sic) place in law enforcement … Don't ask police to ignore what we know. Black gang members from Teaneck commit burglaries in Wyckoff. That's why we check out suspicious black people in white neighborhoods, White kids buy heroin in black NYC neighborhoods."[105] This is common sense. The Chief resigned later that year.

The NJSP on the other hand were not following their instincts. Their problems came to a head following the 1998 shooting of unarmed minority motorists on the New Jersey Turnpike. The following timeline explains their history.

1989: The Middlesex County Public Defender's Office alleges that a high percentage of black, out-of-state motorists are being stopped on the New Jersey Turnpike by the State Police based on their race and no other evidence of wrongdoing.

1991: A State Superior Court Judge says evidence of racial profiling must be reviewed on a case-by-case basis for more than 200 people seeking to have charges dropped because they believe they were unfairly targeted because they were black.

1993: A group of black State Troopers sue State Police claiming they were victims of discrimination and racial hazing because they were denied job transfers, unfairly disciplined to prevent promotion and assigned to jobs far from their homes.

---

[104] Wikipedia

[105] ACLU, *"Email Suggests Wyckoff Police Chief Ordered Racial Profiling"* (March 22, 2016)

1996: A State Superior Court Judge in Gloucester County rules that certain stops made by State Police on the Turnpike from 1988 to 1991 were unconstitutional because they were based solely on the race of occupants. Public defenders in the State raise alarm.

(Gov. Whitman photographed patting down black juvenile, talk about bad timing – the exact date is difficult to determine)

1998: The turning point was when two Troopers fired on a van carrying four young, minority men on the Turnpike wounding three. Though the Troopers contend they were threatened, the incident sparks what will become a massive inquiry into racial profiling by Troopers in the state.

1998: As lawsuits against the State Police pile up, Superintendent Col. Carl Williams insists there is no tolerance for racial discrimination and a Federal Judge finds in one case that "racial incidents were not accidental, sporadic or limited to a few isolated acts."

1998: A group of black ministers in New Jersey demand the State Police halt alleged profile stops and attempt to recruit more minority troopers. Williams again reiterates that profiling on the State's roadways will not be tolerated.

1999: Attorney General Peter Verniero launches an investigation after the Star-Ledger finds minorities made up 75 percent of those arrested on the Turnpike in the first two months of 1997. The force is besieged by allegations of racial profiling.

1999: The Civil Rights Division of the U.S. Justice Department confirms it is investigating allegations that the State Police are illegally targeting minority motorists. Black leaders in New Jersey endorse the review and call for action.

1999: Gov. Christie Whitman fires Williams as superintendent after he tells The Star-Ledger that illegal drug trafficking in the United States could be linked to some minorities. (The NJ Turnpike has always been thought to be a pipeline for drugs and guns coming north).

1999: The Attorney General's Office releases statistics showing that three of four drivers arrested on the Turnpike are minorities.

1999: The Attorney General's Office for the first time says racial profiling "is real – not imagined," a dramatic reversal after years of denying any pattern of wrongdoing. A report recommending a host of changes to the Force follows.

1999: Two troopers are indicted for attempted murder in the 1998 Turnpike shooting.

1999: A federal monitor is appointed to watch over New Jersey's efforts to root out the State Police practice of racial profiling, under a deal to settle a lawsuit by U.S. civil rights officials that charges the force with engaging in "intentional racial discrimination."

2000: The State Police and National Association for the Advancement of Colored People settle claims of racial discrimination in hiring. The Force pledges to attract and retain more minority recruits in the coming decade.

2000: An internal memo shows State Police were aware of profiling in the mid-1990s and attempted to divert the attention of federal investigators away from the problem. Documents later show Verniero also knew years before he launched an investigation.

2001: After the State's admission of racial profiling, the State Police are beset by complaints from Troopers claiming they were discriminated against by the Division.

2002: Two white State Troopers avoided jail by pleading guilty to lesser charges in a turnpike shooting that forced New Jersey and the nation to confront the issue of ethnic profiling.

2003: Superintendent Col. Rick Fuentes confirmed by the State Senate despite criticism for lamenting in a 1997 memo that a drug interdiction program was dismantled when the State came under fire for racial profiling. *(Gov. McGreevy signs legislation that makes it illegal for law enforcement officers to use race, color, religion, ethnicity, handicap, gender, age, or sexual orientation to discriminate against any individual.)*[106]

2006: Despite its 2000 settlement with the NAACP pledging more minority recruitment, statistics show the force is failing to attract qualified black candidates.

---

[106]   Tom Hester, *"Racial profiling is now a crime – State law enacted 5 years after Turnpike case"* The Star ledger, (March 15, 2003), Pg. 11

2009: The U.S. Justice Department ends federal monitoring that stemmed from racial profiling, finding that the State Police have completed significant reforms. *(Governor Jon S. Corzine signed into law the Law Enforcement Professional Standards Act of 2009, which codifies the reforms implemented by the State Police to end racial profiling. The law mandates continued state oversight and monitoring of the State Police, creating an office within the Attorney General's Office that will continue the oversight role that had been performed by federal monitors under the consent decree.)*[107]

2011: The NAACP threatens to revisit 2000 settlement over minority recruitment and hiring after only five black recruits graduate from a class of 123. Statistics show that the number of black troopers fell from 8 percent to 6.4 percent from 2000 to 2011.

2011: Under the command of Major Lewis, the State Police take to cities to build relationships with black leaders and church ministers in order to improvement minority recruitment. Gov. Chris Christie and Attorney General Jeffrey Chiesa make the issue a top priority.

2013: The State Police graduate two of the most diverse classes of new Troopers in State history.

Jan. 8: Major Gerald Lewis files suit against the State Police, claiming he was subjected to a bogus internal investigation, ordered by Fuentes, into who sent an anonymous letter about the Colonel's personal life. Lewis says he was targeted by Fuentes and investigators because he is black and might be chosen as the next Colonel.[108]

2016: A Federal grant provides 1,575 body cams for Troopers.

- Note: The federal government stopped monitoring the State Police for possible racial discrimination more than a decade ago but they are still falling short in key areas. One item was that commanders have failed to regularly sign off on statements

[107] Office of the Attorney General, *"State Police Racial Profiling Decree Dissolved"* Department of Law & Public Safety, (Sept. 21, 2009), OAG Home

[108] Christopher Baxtor, *"Timeline of NJ State Police struggles with racial discrimination"* The Star Ledger, (Jan. 10, 2014), NJ.com

confirming they are abiding by recent reforms. These statements are required by law.[109]

During the height of this mess, I had a difficult time in wrapping my head around this matter. I called in two of my black officers and asked them if racial profiling was going on. They absolutely confirmed it. One of the guys told me he had to leave ten minutes early for work to allow him time to get stopped by the police in another town. I was horrified. There are some things you cannot explain or cure. Eldridge Cleaver[110] said, "If you're not part of the solution, you're part of the problem." All Police Officers need to be part of the solution.

I tend to go along with the thoughts of Leonard Pitts[111] who wrote, "I've spent 11 years writing about race - In that time two frustrating truths have become clear to me. The first is that many white Americans labor under the self-justifying fantasy that racism just up and disappeared 40 years ago. The second is that many black Americans labor under the equally vexing belief that racism explains everything, that it is the all-purpose excuse anytime one of "us" gets in trouble, gets criticized, or just gets rude service in the checkout line."[112] I always said, "Sometimes it has nothing to do with race and sometimes it's all about race." All parties involved need to determine what is going on during a given situation and take the totality of circumstance into consideration before the race card is thrown on the table because once you play that card, it is difficult to recall it. One of the top abuse of power cases, literally the king of brutality incidents, was the Rodney King beating. On March 3, 1991, King was violently beaten by LAPD officers during

---

[109]   Blake Nelson, *"Report: Trooper anti-bias tracking needs correcting"* The Star Ledger, (May, 16, 2016), Pg. A2

[110]   This saying was attributed to Cleaver, writer, activists, and leader of the Black Panther Party, but was originally coined by Vista advertising agency owner, Charles Rosner, or a host of others including the Bible - "Those who are not for us are against us"

[111]   Leonard Garvey Pitts Jr. (born October 11, 1957) is an American commentator, journalist, and novelist. He is a nationally syndicated columnist and winner of the 2004 Pulitzer Prize for Commentary.

[112]   Leonard Pitts, *"Not everything's racial"* amNY.com, (March 21, 2006), pg. 9

his arrest for fleeing and resisting arrest.[113] Four officers took turns and stepped forward and struck a prone suspect on the ground with their batons. They had sufficient manpower to physically overwhelm Mr. King and place him under arrest but they chose not to. A civilian, George Holliday, filmed the incident from his nearby balcony and sent the footage to local news station. The footage clearly showed King being beaten repeatedly, and the incident was covered by news media around the world.[114] Mr. Holliday had offered the footage to the Police first because he felt they needed to see it. They told him to get lost. He went to the news media. Police continue to be stupid.

Everyone was outraged by this incident but it wasn't until a year later on April 29, 1992, when the four Officers were found not guilty of assault with a deadly weapon and excessive force against Mr. King,[115] that the shit really hit the fan. The following days after the verdict marked the beginning of one of the deadliest, most destructive race riots in the nation's history. The riot left 55 people dead and more than 2,300 injured. More than 1,500 buildings were damaged or destroyed with property damage estimated at $1 billion.[116] (1992 dollars)

The point to be made here is that although the actual beating upset the nation, what really pissed off the minority population of Los Angeles was that the white officers got away with it.

The rest of the story goes like this:

The federal government prosecuted a separate civil rights case, obtaining Grand Jury indictments of the four Officers for violations of King's civil rights. Their trial in a Federal District Court ended on April 16, 1993, with two of the Officers being found guilty and sentenced to serve prison terms. The other two were acquitted of the charges. In

---

113   Wikipedia, *Rodney King*

114   Ibid.

115   David A. Love, *"Not all police lessons learned, 20 years after Rodney King"* The Star Ledger, (April, 27, 2012), Pg. 15

116   John Rogers & Amy Taxin, *"Times have changed, but the race riot 20 years ago still haunts L.A."* The Star Ledger, (April 26, 2012), Pg. 6

a separate suit, the City of Los Angeles awarded King $3.8 million in damages. He attempted to start a business, but was not successful.

In 2012, Rodney King was found dead in his swimming pool two months after publishing his memoir; the Coroner found evidence of alcohol and drugs in his system and ruled these and his history of heart problems had likely resulted in an accidental drowning.[117]

---

[117] Wikipedia, *Rodney King*

Chapter Ten

A Higher Standard

"With great power comes great responsibility"

-Uncle Ben[118]

The topic of Racial Profiling can fill volumes, but all I want to say about it here is that when done by law enforcement, it inflicts more harm and absolutely no good. I am usually not on the side of the ACLU because I believe they take things to the extreme and overlook common sense, but I have to agree with their statement: Racial Profiling alienates communities from law enforcement, hinders community policing efforts, and causes law enforcement to lose credibility and trust among the people they are sworn to protect and serve.[119]

---

[118] Uncle Ben is of course was Peter Parker alias Spiderman's Uncle. In 1906, Winston Churchill, the Under-Secretary of the Colonial Office uttered, "where there is great power there is great responsibility". Almost a century before that, in the year 1817, William Lamb, a member of the British parliament was also recorded saying, "the possession of great power necessarily implies great responsibility".

[119] "Racial profiling" aclu.org

Just plain profiling used to be referred to as a 6th sense in police work (Terry) as described in the previous chapter. It's the feeling you develop over time that something isn't right. This is based on years of experience, training, and dealing with numerous people from all walks of life on a day-to-day basis.

There is no room for any type of racism, bigotry, and discrimination in any career or life in general. It is vital to eliminate this behavior in law enforcement because of the power entrusted in the Officers. In the past it was difficult to convict Police Officers because experts say the bar was set higher for them, and there was a general perception of trust in law enforcement.[120]

I have asked every class if Police should be held to a higher standard. They unanimously agree they should. I then ask why. I received one correct answer among thousands of recruits. The answer I was looking for was, because they can fucking kill people. I challenge them to go home and look through the want ads and find another job where you can kill people. There are very few.

I then show them this slide:

We hold these truths to be self-evident, ***that all men are created equal, that they are endowed by their Creator with certain unalienable Rights, that among these are Life, Liberty and the pursuit of Happiness.****--That to secure these rights, Governments are instituted among Men, deriving their just powers from the consent of the governed,*[121]

Police are allowed to violate the Constitution of the United States under proper circumstances. Police can take a life, they can take your liberty, and they certainly reduce happiness on a sliding scale depending on the type of interaction. Approximately 1,000 people die during confrontations with the Police every year. This is a relatively high number but rather low when you consider the greater number of chuckleheads that do stupid things, like point guns at police, attack police with or without weapons, commit heinous crimes, and violently resist arrest. One

[120] Alex Napoliello, *"Why conviction is difficult when police use force"* The Star Ledger, (June18, 2020) Pg.1
[121] Thomas Jefferson, *"The Declaration of Independence"* (July 4, 1776)

of the biggest complaints is that the Police shoot a lot of black people. According to the Washington Post[122], in 2019, 1004 people were killed by police, 371 were white, 236 where black, and a weapon was involved in 93% of the incidents (928). Yes, disproportionately to total population, more blacks are killed by Police than whites. There are far too numerous issues that come into play that attributes to this disparity. The point I am making here is that there is a lot of power that must be controlled, guided, supervised, and then reviewed, then adjusted or eliminated.

A lower form of abuse of power is similar to bullying for adults, known as entitlement. This is commonly found among the rich and famous, who also hold the power. Entitlement can creep into law enforcement mainly because of the power but without the fame. You see it all the time with actors and the Hollywood elite, whose contribution to society is to dress up and pretend. Don't get me wrong, I am a fan of entertainment, I don't believe any of them are better than me. They have a talent. The other large group is professional athletes, whose contribution to society is catching a ball, or running really fast, etc. This group has also worked extremely hard to achieve their physical status and I appreciate their efforts. They are people that have done well for themselves and you would think that they should be better people for having been so fortunate. But there are the few that abuse this fame and resulting power like spoiled children. It is not pretty. The #Metoo Movement evolved because of, or in spite, of these people. Many powerful men subscribed to the Tony Montana Scarface School of Abuse which claimed, "first you get the money, then you get the power, then you get the women." Many have fallen and many others have not yet learned that lesson yet.

Comedian, Steve Martin once said, "It was nice to get special treatment. Avoid lines at the airport, always a table available at the best restaurants. You get used to this type of treatment." The problem is that some people expect this treatment all the time, wherever they go. When any of the above famous people pulls out the entitlement card, it plays out as disgusting and cheap. The abusers always use the standard line, "do you know who I am," if they don't get their way or their power is challenged.

---

[122]   Washingtonpost.com/graphics/2019/national/police-shootings-2019

I was going to mention the infamous Bridgegate scandal where our trusted top New Jersey officials had an out-of-control temper tantrum and attempted to exact political revenge upon the Mayor of Fort Lee for declining to support the re-election of then Gov. Christie. They closed two of the three lanes to the George Washington Bridge on the first day of school, September 9, 2013, thus causing massive traffic and gridlock throughout the town, impacting tens of thousands of people in two states. Why would they do this? Because they thought they could get away with it. Who would possibly notice shutting down one of the world's busiest bridges?

I was going to mention this incident but as I write this the Supreme Court tossed out the convictions. The Governor was never charged but this caper played a major role in his failed 2016 Presidential bid. (He will be back in 2024 because we all have short memories). The Supreme Court, however, said the actions of the former Christie aides, though possibly corrupt, did not constitute a federal crime.[123] Justice Elena Kagan wrote. "The evidence the jury heard, no doubt shows wrongdoing – deception, corruption, abuse of power."[124] This is of course is considered a win in political circles.

Convicted Port Authority executive, Bill Baroni, told the Federal Judge at his sentencing in 2017 that, "he lost his moral bearings when he was sucked into the cult of the Gov. Chris Christie's political ambition."[125] This poor frog never saw it coming as the water rapidly heated up to a rolling boil. Gov. Christie later stated that this may have changed the course of history. We will never know how the world would have turned out if he had become President.

A very good example of entitlement occurred on March 31, 2018, when Tenafly Police Officers stopped a vehicle for tinted windows, a simple nonmoving equipment violation. The registration was also expired.

---

[123] Ted Sherman, *"Convictions tossed in GWB lane-closing case"* The Star Ledger, (Ma 8, 2020), Pg. 1

[124] Tom Moran, *"Will Christie's sins against the people of N.J. be forgotten?"* The Star Leger, ((May 10, 2020) Pg. D1

[125] Ted, Sherman, *"Baroni gets 18 months in resentencing"* The Star Ledger, (March 29, 2017), n.p.

The mother of one of the passengers showed up at the scene and handed one of the Officers a business card identifying herself as a Port Authority Commissioner. She also exhibited a full-size gold badge in a badge wallet that had the same identification printed on it. (Ironically, she was also the chair of the Governance & Ethics Committee for the PA). She flashed her PA badge and attempted to bully the Police Officers and then cursed at them. All of this caught on dash cam video. The Officer stated, *"the Commissioner then began a line of questioning in a demanding nature. Based on her demeanor, the tone of voice, the way she presented herself and the way she was attempting to misappropriately use her professional position to gain authority in this situation, the Officer advised her to speak with the driver of the vehicle for more information...she became further enraged and began using profanity. 'Don't call me Miss, I'm Commissioner.' She continued to speak with a condescending tone, using profanity once again. She stated "you're an ass" as well as "look at that smug ass look on your face" and "You may shut the fuck up." She told the Police she had all of their information from their badges and threatened to complain about them to the higher ups. "I will be talking to the Chief of Police and I will be speaking to the Mayor," she warned[126]."*

Luckily the Officers maintained their composure and acted professionally in the face of total ignorance and pure entitlement. An investigation was begun and revealed the Commissioner's conduct was profoundly disturbing and violated the newly enacted Code of Ethics. She resigned immediately upon hearing of the investigation.[127]

That should have been the end of the matter but then they went looking for bird shit in the cuckoo clock. In August of 2019, Gov. Murphy signed a Law that prohibited the Port Authority of New York and New Jersey, New Jersey Transit, and municipalities and counties in the State from issuing badges that could be used to garner favor to non-law enforcement elected officials.[128] One entitled asshole ruined it for hundreds of others who were playing by the rules.

---

[126] Amy Kuperinsky, *"Tale of P.A. tape needed to be told, say top cop"* The Star Ledger, (April 26, 2018), pg. 1 – along with a compilation of follow up articles
[127] Ted Sherman, *"Ethics chair quits in shadow of investigation"* The Star Ledger, (no date), Pg. 1
[128] Larry Higgs, *"Gov. signs bill to outlaw badges for some officials"* The Star Ledger, (August 10, 2019), Pg. A3

Wait, we are not done yet. The media attacked the need for the restriction on tinted windows.[129] Yes, because tinted windows was the problem here. Please go to YouTube and watch the full video: Port Authority commissioner confronts Police during N.J. traffic stop. I take great pleasure in the fact that this moment will live forever.

Sometimes Police have to go out of their way not to show entitlement or favoritism. In October of 2011, Lodi Police Chief Vincent Caruso ordered an Officer to ticket his wife when she double-parked while dropping off their son at school. The Chief paid $54 to make sure no one could say his wife was above the law. When asked how things were at home, he said, "They're okay, not great, but okay."

I have told my recruits not to be an asshole. That includes flashing the **Badge Americard** (don't leave home without it) for special favors. I can't say I am innocent in this area. I had a heavy foot (hazards of the job) and have been pulled over for speeding (not Death Race speeding) on several occasions, once in Pennsylvania, and displayed my identification. I would never have argued if the Trooper had given me a summons. I did collect a souvenir in Utah and paid the $92 for improper lane change. (I was innocent like everyone else). My son is a Police Officer and proudly displays my paid $25 parking ticket from his Department at his desk. The public often believes that Police think they are entitled by the way Police react during an interaction with the public. This problem exists because Police are under the delusional misconception that the public will not only listen to them but also follow all of their directions. The Officer takes any violation or challenge to their instructions or orders as a personal affront and insult to their sworn authority. To take a quote from Super Chicken,[130] "You knew the job was dangerous when you took it." It is also frustrating as hell.

For a long time this was thought to be a testosterone issue because all cops were males. This "How Dare You Syndrome" continued after

---

[129]   Larry Higgs, *"In wake of P.A. fracas, a look at tinted-windows regulations"* The Star Ledger, (May 7, 2018), n.p.

[130]   Wikipedia, Super Chicken is a segment that ran on the animated television series George of the Jungle. It was produced by Jay Ward and Bill Scott, who earlier had created the Rocky and Bullwinkle cartoons. It debuted September 9, 1967, on ABC.

females started to populate more and more Departments. Women now suffer the same indignations during confrontations as males. Women may be more offended because they may feel they are being dismissed because they are women. However, I am not a woman and have no real proof of this so don't kill me for it. I do not speak for women. I am 100% pro female cop. Police have a clear understanding of the rules and how they should be followed and get out of joint when the rules are not followed accordingly (This unfortunately carries over to their personal life). The Officer usually starts the conversation. They are met with denial, hostility, or are ignored (possibly worse than hostility). The Officer reacts to this behavior. The key is not to overreact. The most common interaction occurs during a motor vehicle stop. The Officer tells the driver they were speeding. The answer is, "No I wasn't." The driver must be right and the Officer is making the entire thing up.

When asked to step out of the vehicle, a common answer heard is "Fuck you." At this point the Officer needs to take a breath because deep down in their hearts they want to drag the driver out of the small vent window.[131] The Officer's mental state is not entitlement and that they are better than the public, but the power concept is present. The Officer knows he/she has the right and the authority to make such demands of the driver and they unrealistically expect compliance. How dare they refuse the Police!

Let me interject a quick war story. A 'request' was passed down to patrol from my Chief (which is considered an order) to issue summonses for studded snow tires on vehicles after the allowed time period (no one uses studded tires anymore with the advancement of all-wheel drive). The way you can tell someone has these tires is you can hear the metal hitting the road surface. I tried to keep my Chief happy and proceeded to stop a utility pickup truck for this violation.

I approached the driver and requested the required paperwork and advised the driver I would be issuing a no point summons for the equipment violation. As I returned to my patrol vehicle the driver drove

---

[131] They did away with vent windows because of the EPA that's right they figured you could get better fuel mileage because the vent causes wind drag so they mandated no more vent windows. They were too small to get a human body through them.

off. I had the driver's credentials but no one flees from an equipment violation unless something else is going on. I radioed my status and that I would be pursuing the vehicle.

The chase went on for over a mile before I forced the vehicle to a stop. I again approached the driver and now informed him he was under arrest for eluding Police. He stated his truck was his home and he wasn't leaving it as he firmly grasped the steering wheel with both hands. I requested a backup unit to assist me. A fellow Officer arrived, and I advised him the driver was under arrest and was refusing to exit the vehicle. The rocket scientist behind the wheel neglected to roll up his window, which I thought would make extraction easier. We were able to open the driver's door but it took some effort for the two of us to remove the driver, as he had forearms like Popeye.

The three of us wound up rolling around on the roadway before the driver was handcuffed and placed in my patrol vehicle. At that point, my backup officer asked me what the driver had done. My answer was, of course, studded snow tires. During the tussle there were no punches thrown by the good or the bad guy. It was just a really strong refusal. The suspect counter-charged us with aggravated assault that was thrown out in Court. My only charges against me in 28 years was because of studded snow tires! (The Chief is an asshole.)

Vehicle stop scenarios plays out far more times than life and death struggles or shoot outs. This is the incident that gets replayed over and over again at family dinners, parties or other social gatherings. I tell my recruits that they may stop a thousand drivers and not remember most of them. A driver may get stopped only once and will remember that encounter for the rest of his or her life. There is an old saying in business, "Give a customer good service and they will tell someone. Give them bad service and they will tell everyone." It is paramount that each Officer use their great power, legally, sparingly, reasonably, and with good conscience.

Chapter Eleven

Reasonable & Necessary

"It is reasonable that everyone who asks justice should do justice."

-Thomas Jefferson

I have covered topics including plain stupid actions that may have started out as a joke and then gone terribly wrong, bad decisions, blatant criminal activity, racial bias, and entitlement. One thing in law enforcement that is more visible than all these others is brutality. Police brutality is the use of excessive and/or unnecessary force by personnel affiliated with law enforcement duties when dealing with suspects and civilians.[132] The majority of Police interactions (estimated to be over 100 million per year) are completed with no confrontation or any physical contact. Only the bad ones are news worthy. I have already pointed out that arrests are not pretty. Imagine a calf roping at a rodeo. It is almost uncomfortable to watch as the small animal is lassoed, falls to the ground, and then struggles for its freedom.

---

[132]   Wikipedia, "*Police brutality in the United States*"

During an arrest, or sometimes to a lesser degree, to calm a person or restrict their movement for safety reasons, some amount of force must be used to accomplish this goal. The key is in the amount used. The New Jersey Use of Force Policy states: A law enforcement officer may use physical force or mechanical force when the officer reasonably believes it is immediately necessary at the time, basically to meet and overcome the force being used against them.

In situations where law enforcement officers are justified in using force, the utmost restraint should be exercised. The use of force should never be considered routine. In determining to use force, the law enforcement officer shall be guided by the principle that the degree of force employed in any situation should be only that reasonably necessary. Law enforcement officers should exhaust all other reasonable means before resorting to the use of force. It is the policy of the State of New Jersey that law enforcement officers will use only that force which is objectively **reasonable and necessary.**[133]

The last two words of the previous paragraph has been and will continue to be debated among juries until the end of time. All the answers to all the questions regarding Police actions were supposed to have been supplied by the all-seeing body cam. Regrettably, they were not. Body cams have raised more questions. (Was it a touchdown?)

The police often make an attempt to police themselves but often it appears like they make an attempt for appearances sake to please the public and not to find the answers to real problems. ***If the police refuse or otherwise fail to police themselves, experience has shown there are many other individuals and organizations who will do it for them...***[134] On March 20, 2018 the New Jersey Attorney General issued directive No. 2018-3, which requires all law enforcement agencies to adopt and implement an "Early Warning System." The largest Police Union in the State, NJPBA, felt the new EWS was purposely designed to target cops in situations where the employer cannot prove any wrongdoing in court. The EWS is triggered by categories such

---

[133]   N..J Attorney General Use of Force Policy, Revised 2000
[134]   The Center for American and International Law

as; conduct which indicates potentially escalating risk of harm to the public, the agency and/or the Officer, even though there is no proof of actual misconduct.[135]

In any small to medium size Police Department, you don't need a score care to tell you who the assholes are. There are no part-time assholes. They are always assholes.

In 2019, NJ Advance Media conducted a 16-month investigation to produce what they referred to as *The Force Report*. They did an exhaustive job going through 72,609 documents that covered a five-year period. It is an interesting read and can be found online at NJ.com/force.[136] Anyone can look up their favorite Officer in any community to see what despicable deeds these men and women have been up to. The report would have been a great tool had it not been introduced by a biased media with sub articles like: *Ways police are legally allowed to harm another person.* The media know no one wants to read about the White Hats. Everyone wants to know about the bad guys because it is more interesting getting the dirt on someone, especially someone that holds more power that oneself. That is what sells newspapers. This is a hard lesson to be learned if you ever get in a jam; you are fresh meat for the grinder. Reports should be based upon the facts and then let the reader make up their own mind.

Please don't misinterpret my hostility towards *The Force Report* as disapproving. All governmental agencies should be reviewed and accountable to the public especially law enforcement for reasons I have already covered. This study was long overdue and, as the writers half joked, they did the job for the Attorney General. What upsets me is what they left out of the report.

According to the US Bureau of Justice Statistics 2008 Census of State and Local Law Enforcement Agencies, New Jersey had 550 law enforcement agencies in 21 counties employing 33,704 sworn Police Officers. This produces innumerable variables in countless situations.

---

[135] Peter Paris, *"A warning about the Early Warning System"* New Jersey COPS, (No date)

[136] Craig McCarthy & Stephen Stirling, *"Police System Under Review"* The Star Ledger,(Dec. 16, 2018), Pg.1

There are over 500,000 LEOs in United States with approximately 10% or 50,000 Officers assaulted every year with an average of 120 deaths per year - every year.[137] Another factoid they left out is that no one wants to be arrested. In my almost 28 years as a LEO, I have never witnessed anyone say to another Officer or to myself, "Why thank you Officer, I would be happy to put those handcuffs on, here let me assist you so you don't get dirty." I have seen four large Officers attempt to subdue a mentally handicapped patient who was a 100-pound, four foot nothing, petite female with the supernatural power of Linda Blair in the Exorcist. The suspect was taken to the floor and then she proceeded to lift the Officers off her.

What the report does admit is that the current Use of Force Reports system itself is flawed. It is not uniform among all agencies. If a Department submits a lot or reports, does that mean they are overly abusive or just really good at reporting incidents. The opposite holds true for Departments with low numbers. Are they perfect angels or bad at reporting?

The simple fact is that if there was a Use of Force Report filed it does not indicate if force was warranted or if there was excessive force used. I was proud of the fact that in all my years making arrests, I never injured anyone requiring hospitalization or even stiches. A couple of people may have bled a little but those things happen. I'm sorry to say I worked in an era before the Use of Force reports so you will have to take my word for it.

If a Department has a proactive Officer, he or she is going to have more arrests, resulting in more UOF reports, and more citizen complaints. There was an old saying, "If no one is complaining about you then you are not doing your job." I'm not totally stupid, of course there are abusive cops. Of course, there are racist cops. Yearly reviews should weed out the bad ones and get rid of them immediately. There is no place in law enforcement for a 1930's cop mentality in today's world.

Let me explain a couple more reasons that no one wants to talk about, why cops sometimes use excessive force. Number one reason is that they have **no other choice**. They do not possess the skills to handle a larger or stronger or sometimes deranged person with super human strength.

---

[137] Wikipedia

Many times, the suspect is all of the above. I was Director of Security for a hospital after I retired and personally witnessed seven Police Officers deliver a 6'10" suspect that was high on PCP. You couldn't ask for a worse combination. They happily turned him over to my lesser equipped and sufficiently smaller staff. And then on other occasions, Police may deal with a 100-pound five foot nothing, petite female. A recruit graduates from the Police Academy at what may well be the peak of their physical conditioning. It is all downhill from there. Many Departments do not have a physical fitness standard for Officers once they get off probation. These Officers are human beings and deteriorate at the same or faster rate as the average office worker living in a cubicle. There is no incentive for Police Officers to stay in shape. They must be self-motivated.

We had a beautiful new gym in the basement of our Police Department. I approached possibly our strongest Officer, a power lifter, in our department who held the rank of Lieutenant and proposed a physical fitness program that would include some time off at the end of a shift that would allow the Officers to work out. I thought this would be a good investment in our Officers. I believed I had an ally with a lifelong gym rat. I did not. He provided numerous counter arguments why we couldn't. Don't try it, just deny it. Law enforcement hates change. A few Officers used the gym but for the most part it went to waste. It was totally up to the individual if they were going to survive a violent physical confrontation.

"When you are not practicing, remember, someone somewhere is, and when you meet him, he is going to win!" - Ed Mcauley[138]

The second reason for excessive force is that Officers are ill equipped for the job. The weapons of choice for the average Police Officer is a baton (nightstick/PR24) and a gun. (A) you beat them or (B) you shoot them. If you are lucky, they let you carry (C) pepper spray (also known as mace). I heard a story of a bad guy taking the pepper spray away from an Officer and spraying into his own mouth like a breath freshener.

---

[138] Wikipedia, Ed Macauley was a standout basketball player who led St. Louis University to an NCAA Championship and later won an NBA Championship with the St. Louis Hawks.

Some people are immune (unlike myself with the double homicidal range instructor Sergeant).

New Jersey is the most densely populated State and yet we were the **LAST** State to authorize the use of stun guns by law enforcement Officers. A stun gun is a proven effective non-lethal weapon[139] (but not the answer to all prayers). Why would a State with some of the toughest gun laws on the books, and strong commitment to lower police shootings, while maintaining positive community relations, oppose a non-lethal weapon? Because so few Officers had listed stun guns as a type of force, this statistic was not included in *The Force Report* database. One non-lethal alternative presently used is a 40mm impact munition. This is a large, high-speed projectile. It is basically a nerf gun on steroids. The medical journal *BMJ Open* published documented reports of its use. There have been over 2,000 people injured since 1990 with this weapon. 300 people have suffered a permanent disability and 53 have died.[140] The dying part cancels the non-lethal classification. Again, it comes down to training, which there is minimal. No one should be shot in the face with something that could fracture your skull and cause the loss of an eye. There has to be clear rules of engagement. During the summer of 2020, the Police were attempting to do what they could, or were allowed to do, against riotous mobs that were using anything they could get their hands on as weapons against the Police. Rioters have no rules.

My phone has more capabilities than the NASA computers that launched John Glenn into space but no one can come up with a better solution to safely subdue a hostile person. For God's sake, watch any science fiction movie. They have already stolen many ideas from the original Star Trek series. No one is trying.

There has been no major breakthroughs in non-lethal technology, within the last 20 years. I'm sorry, let me amend that statement to, no one is listening. Some people are trying. The Buffalo Grove Police Department tested a device made by Wrap Technologies. This is a handheld remote

---

[139] Robert Farago, "NJ Finally Approves TASERs For the Police" The Truthabutguns.com, (Oct. 17, 2011)
[140] Lee Cowan reporting, *"Police tactics that are considered non-lethal force"* (Aug. 30, 2020) CBS This Morning S220, EP 830

restraint device called the BolaWrap, that fires an 8-foot Kevlar tether at a range of up to 25 feet.[141] No one has ever heard about this.[142] The third reason that Police Officers use excessive force is that they are undertrained. The academies do a great job but they are under strict requirements to get as much done in a restricted period of time. Recruits undergo a grueling 20 weeks of training and come out with a "deer-in-the-headlights" look about them. Do you know why? Because as Puff Daddy stated, "It's all about the Benjamins." It costs money to build a Police Officer. Money that municipalities do not have nor are they willing to spend.

The New Jersey A.G. stated, "Policing has such a wide variety of things to train on that you can spend an enormous amount of time and money on training. It would be so oppressively expensive and costly, you wouldn't be able to maintain it, so you have to pick what you're going to train."[143]

Here's an eye opener for you:

It is estimated to cost \$350,000 to \$500,000 to train a single Navy SEAL. To keep a single Navy SEAL operational and deployable overseas it costs somewhere around \$1,000,000 per year. SEAL training is six weeks longer than a police academy and but these people come out as SEALS.[144]

I believe since the Police are the occupational force of the United States (not in a conspiracy way), they should be as well trained to step up and meet a threat as well as be prepared to de-escalate the situation if at all possible. They are not. After 20 weeks of basic training, an Officer should be fluent in Spanish and possess some reasonable skill in martial arts. They do not.

Most police officers are competent in firearms but are far from expert shots. They are only required to qualify twice a year for a few

---

[141]   Christopher Carbone, "Police officers test new restraint technology" (August 13, 2018)

[142]   BoloWrap is currently used in 120 police departments across the United States – there are close to 18,000 departments.

[143]   Alex Napoliello, *"Working towards a better police system"* The Star Ledger, (June 4, 2020), Pg. 6

[144]   Google

hours with a weapon that could kill someone. This is literally a tool of life and death and given almost no weight in the entire scope of training, and this is their Second Choice to use against a bad guy. The general public believes what they see on TV and in the movies and think a cop can shoot a weapon out of someone's hand or "wound someone in the leg" (Joe Biden). The average Officer is lucky if they could hit center mass of a grown adult body in a close-up gun battle.

As a range instructor I attempted to make training more realistic. I pulled a patrol vehicle onto the outdoor course. I then had the Officers run a short distance to the vehicle, take appropriate cover behind it, and then shoot at the target over the hood. This was to simulate the raised heart rate they would experience in a gun battle and stress the importance of proper safety by protecting themselves behind a vehicle (cover).

The results were as I expected. I got my ass chewed out for endangering municipal equipment (the car) and was forbidden to ever think again (There is a pattern here). My argument that it would be better for them to shoot the car during training fell on deaf ears. Law enforcement hates change or innovative thinking.

Police are trained *enough*. Not to exceed but to meet the *minimum standards* of legal requirements to keep municipalities clear of law suits. When an Officer screws up or kills someone, they pull out the mounds of training records and show that the Officer was not taught to do that. How has that worked out for them so far?

Every year they add another vital course to the already bulging curriculum like, "Be Nice to People." They should hand out Robert Fulghum's[145] book, *All I Really Need to Know I Learned in Kindergarten*, and save a couple hundred hours of training:

1. Don't take things that aren't yours.
2. Don't hit people.
3. Hold hands, stick together.
4. Share.

---

[145] Robert Fulghum is a writer, philosopher, and public speaker, but he has also worked as a cowboy, a folksinger, an IBM salesman, a professional artist, a parish minister, a bartender, a teacher of drawing and painting, and a father.

5. Live a balanced life.
6. Take a nap every afternoon.
7. Listen.
8. Treat everyone the way you want to be treated.
9. Things change and come to an end.
10. Be aware of wonder.

To the authors of The Force Report, I say, good job. It was a long time coming but don't stop there. Find out the "Why" before you tell people what to think. Then find an alternative to the use of force. You will be heroes. The cops are really doing the best they can with what they have to work with, which isn't much.

If life were not hard enough for law enforcement, they have rewritten the narrative on any (legal or otherwise) use of force. The politically correct term to use now is Police Violence! This changes the entire dynamics of every police/citizen encounter. This indicates that the Officer was in the wrong by the very nature of a physical encounter. It will not be long before they change the name of the report to indicate violence instead of force.

The United States Supreme Court has already weighed in on this issue.

The Court explained that, "As in other Fourth Amendment contexts... the "reasonableness" inquiry in an excessive force case is an objective one: the question is whether the Officers' actions are 'objectively reasonable' in light of the facts and circumstances confronting them, without regard to their underlying intent or motivation." The Court also cautioned, "The "reasonableness" of a particular use of force must be judged from the perspective of a reasonable officer on the scene, rather than with the 20/20 vision of hindsight."

The Court then outlined a non-exhaustive list of factors for determining when an officer's use of force is objectively reasonable: "the severity of the crime at issue," "whether the suspect poses an immediate threat to the safety of the officers or others," and "whether he is actively resisting arrest or attempting to evade arrest by flight."[146]

Sounds simple enough!

---

[146] Wikipedia, *Graham v. Connor*, 490 U.S. 386 (1989)

Chapter Twelve

The Cost of Doing Business

"The buck stops here."

-Harry Truman

In New Jersey, a municipal budget can be broken down as follows: ½ of the money collected by taxes goes to the Board of Education, ¼ to County Government, and ¼ left over to run all of the remaining municipal department services. This leaves a very small piece to be spent on law enforcement. The problem lies in want versus need. Everyone wants a safe community but are hesitant to pay the price for it. On the other hand, the general public will spare no expense for education, because *it is for the children*! The Police are considered a necessary evil. We really don't want them, but we know in our hearts that we need them. Now there is a movement to "Defund" the Police, or do away with them all together. Let's see how that goes. Al Sharpton, of all people, stated, "Defunding the NYPD is "something a Latte Liberal may go for as they sit around the Hamptons discussing this as an academic problem. But people living on the ground need proper policing."[147]

For some reason the media hates for Police (and teachers) to make a decent living, in one of the highest cost of living States in the nation. I began my career in 1977. My salary was approximately $6.30/hour, before taxes. They would pay a flat fee of $25.00 to appear in court when you were off duty, even if you spent the entire day there. Then if you were really lucky you would come back to work the midnight shift with little or no sleep. It wasn't until the 1990s that police started to earn a decent buck for working shifts around the clock, weekends, and holidays, oh, and risking their lives.

Every so often the media drags out the salary statistics that are public record and now searchable on your home computers, as if police salaries are a deep dark secret, protected by the Knights Templar. The media does it to piss off the taxpayers and to sell newspapers. In 2010, the Star Ledger ran a series, similar to the Use of Force series, to demonstrate how taxpayers were getting ripped off. They called it, surprisingly, *The High Cost of Jersey Police,*[148] but they were not trying to lead you with the headline, or anything like that. They did make some good points.

The median salary for the 25,525 municipal cops in New Jersey (2010), not including overtime pay was $90,672. A Star Ledger analysis showed that the average municipal cop in N.J. was paid 80% more than the average resident. In addition, police tend to be paid the best in small towns with little crime.[149] (Because bigger cities always run in the red due to astronomical costs for everything.)

I would like to comment on these statements. First off, all salaries of all municipal and state employees are legally negotiated in agreed upon contracts. The cops are not hoodwinking anyone. Municipalities do not pay more than they can afford to pay. This is not a giveaway

---

[147] Kenneth Garger, *"Al Sharpton says latte liberals want to defund the police"* nypost. com, (Sept. 8, 2020)
[148] Chris Megerian & Sean Sposito, *"The High Cost of Jersey Police"* Star Ledger, (Spt. 19, 2010), Pg. 1
[149] Ibid

sweepstakes. There are no surprises hidden in the contract. They are printed in very identifiable black and white in public documents.

These salaries are honestly earned wages paid, for a typical 2,080-hour year. The U.S. Bureau of Labor Statistics (BLS) claims that in the fourth quarter of 2019, the median income for a full-time wage or salary worker on a weekly basis was $936. For a 40-hour work week, this translates to a yearly income of approximately $48,672.[150] The average N.J. police officer is making almost twice as much as the average citizen. Everything is relative. I don't complain that my dentist makes too much money.

- Note – I worked for an upper-class community. Most of the kids attending the public high school drove better cars than the cops. My guess is that their parents discouraged them from entering law enforcement. I chose that path.

I also agree that cops in tough cities work a great deal harder than suburban cops in small communities. This is an injustice caused by the higher costs for cities to operate. This is a matter of choice. People choose their own career and where they wish to perform that job. On a side note – we had a few inner cities guys come on board to our suburban department. They had a difficult time adjusting.

Not only does the media look at police salaries in disgust, they paint a criminal picture when you add in overtime. Police Officers who really hustle can almost double their base salary by working on their off-time. This is not free money. The Officer had to spend twice as much time at work, away from their family, ignoring their own recreational time and personal health, all the while exposing themselves to all the dangers of the job. When I had my two sons in college, I would finish my eight-hour day shift and then work another eight hours performing security duty at the local hospital emergency room. Did I enjoy the 16-hour day? No, but I did it for my boys and when they graduated, they had no student debt because that's what cops do. I didn't steal this money.

---

[150] Steve Fiorillo, "*What is the Average Income in the U.S.?*" thestreet.com, (Feb. 3, 2019)

Police Director, Joseph Santiago said, "You pay a cop to deal with the stuff you don't want to deal with." The public not only doesn't want to deal with most of this shit, they don't want to know anything about it.

In the *anonymous* editorial, the brave reporter states, "We already knew New Jersey Police Officers were the highest paid in the country but now we've learned two more *startling facts*: They make even more than we thought, and cops who earn the most money have the <u>cushiest jobs</u>. They work in towns with the least amount of crime."[151] The point that our reporting friend neglected to mention was even though they have less crime than bigger cities, they still have the same type of crime.

Please enlighten my fellow Officers who have been dragged down the street by a drunk driver, experienced an arrested subject rip out the metal cage in the Police car and beat them with it, fought for their life during a struggle for the Officers weapon, or been rear- ended by one vehicle and pushed head on into an oncoming tractor trailer. Two of my fellow Officers were struck by cars while directing traffic by inattentive drivers; one almost lost his leg and the other and suffered permanent brain injury causing her to retire on disability. One fine lad intentionally drove a stolen car head on into an approaching Police vehicle sending the Officer to the hospital.

Officers in my department responded to rapes, robberies, assaults (one involving a woman being shot point-blank in the chest with a flare gun), gruesome suicides, horrific motor vehicle accidents, numerous deaths of all ages (including children), and violent domestic violence incidents that would often turn very ugly.

We handled hundreds of emotionally disturbed persons over the years (seriously, some were batshit crazy – I know this is not politically correct, but they were). I had to watch one person we had brought to the hospital for an evaluation. After waiting most of the day for a psychiatrist, because it was a holiday, the doctor interviewed the patient and came out of the room and said to me, "That guy is fucking crazy." I told him I knew that five hours ago and I didn't have to pay for medical

---

[151]   Star Ledger

school. Gee, was it the fact that he was walking around town naked, or that he was talking to dinosaurs, that gave it away?

I was attacked by just an average guy with a hunting knife because he was stopped for speeding by another Officer. We also worked in every type of weather condition including hurricanes, heat waves, and subzero temperatures 24/7/365. This all sounds like a cushy job to me. All this time while the author of the editorial braved paper cuts and spilled coffee in his nice temperature-controlled office. My goodness, I hope he is doing alright.

So, the media attacks a person's choice to protect and serve, and risk his or her life for perfect strangers. A choice open to anyone, even reporters. They look down upon the Officers working their butts off with overtime, speeding up the burn out process. They also hate the Officer receiving fair compensation with a pension after 25 years or more of service. The scoundrel!

A legal pension is the ultimate, slap in the face and insult to the taxpayer according to our brave media. The best part of their indignation comes when the retired Officer continues to work another job after retirement. This is considered double dipping, stealing, being a welfare cheat, and fraud. Many Officers do not pay into Social Security or if they do, they are hit with the Windfall Elimination Provision or super penalty, that reduces any fully earned Social Security payment by more than half. They also did not have the benefit of a 401K plan, profit-sharing program, or yearly bonus. Has anyone checked out the benefits of Congress? The House of Representatives has averaged 146.7 "legislative days" a year since 2001, according to records kept. That's about one day of work every two and a half days. The Senate on the other hand, was in session an average of 165 days a year over the same time period.[152] Now there is a scam!

The new game in town is to eliminate the pension payout for bad behavior thus saving the municipality more cash. Besides all the shenanigans I have covered, they may be expanding the no-no items

---

[152]   Tom Murse, "How many days a year Congress works" thoughtco.co, (Feb. 3. 2020)

to include harassment, sexual assault and lewdness to the list. In the long run, if a retiree lives long enough, this could add up to millions of dollars forfeited. This is a far more severe penalty to pay than your average Joe getting jammed up.

Now add the peripheral costs of lawsuits and settlements due to bad or criminal behavior by The Finest. Let us look at the big daddy of all Police Departments, the NYPD. In 2018, taxpayers spent a whopping $230 million to pay off 6,472 lawsuit settlements. And this was **down** 32% from the previous year.[153] Communities are more willing to pay out a settlement (no matter who is in the right) instead of gamble a jury awarded decision that could be exponentially more in costs. Everyone knows this, including lawyers and the bad guys. Sue everyone and see what sticks. In September of 2020, the City of Louisville, Kentucky agreed to pay $12 million to the family of Breonna Taylor[154], who was shot by Police while they were executing no-knock warrant in a narcotics investigation even though a Grand Jury failed to indict any of the Officers involved for her murder. The case is still under investigation. The Louisville Metro Police declined to comment on the award.

Side note: Since 1997, Congress' Office of Compliance has paid more than $17 million for 264 settlements and awards to federal employees for violations of various employment rules including sexual harassment.[155] These are the same people that preach to us and make laws regarding bad behavior. We are never told about these incidents or who was involved.

My favorite lawsuit was when a juvenile threw a wire onto the power lines of a New Jersey Transit electric train. A 50,000-volt, lightning bolt

---

[153]　Graham Rayman & Clayton Guse, *"NYC spent $230M on NYPD settlements last year: report"* Daily News, (April 15, 2019)dailynews.com

[154]　Christina Carrega, Mark Morales, Eric Levenson, *"Louisville has settled Breonna Taylor's wrongful death lawsuit for $12 million"* CNN, (Sept. 15, 2020)

[155]　Phillip Bump, *"Over the past 20 years, Congress has paid $17.2 million in settlements"* The Washington Post, (Nov. 17, 2017), washingtonpost.com

shot back into the boy but miraculously did not kill him. I was off duty but responded to the scene to find the boy still smoking, alive on the ground. I told the new Sergeant in charge to save everything because this was going to be a big one. It was!

The boy's mother came into headquarters the following Monday to pick up a copy of the report. I politely inquired as to the boy's condition and she immediately started yelling at me and accused me of a cover up. I didn't know there was anything to cover up. It was pretty clear that her son was an idiot. A very lucky idiot. I then politely threw her out of the Department. I believe he settled for a couple million dollars from NJT. My City was once again dropped from the suit of the boy who trespassed on private property and almost electrocuted himself. The Darwin Principal failed again.

Internal lawsuits are as prevalent as attacks from the public. I always said the only person that is satisfied with a promotion is the person that was promoted. The others sue for sexual or racial bias, improper testing, political interference or nepotism. Unfortunately, many times the person suing is correct.

The winner in many stupid categories was a Department where Officers sued their supervisor for repeatedly assaulting them with a large dildo, affectionately named Big Blue. You can't make this stuff up. Cops do dumb shit, often document it, then disseminate it. The public has had enough and they refuse to pay for it any longer. Can you blame them?

This was blatantly clear when on September 18, 2020, the Borough of Mountainside approved a $2.45 million settlement to resolve the previously mentioned claims of a hostile work environment at the Police Department, including the use of a sex toy.[156]

Other civil suits filed against police departments include:[157]

---

[156] Nick Muscavage, *"NJ police settle for $2.4 million over alleged sex toy harassment"* Bridgewater Courier News, (Sept. 29, 2020), mycentraljersey.com

[157] Southwestern Law Enforcement Institute, Center for Law Enforcement Ethics (1997)

- Failure to train as we discussed before.
- Negligent hiring. Basically, you hire someone that can't do the job (nepotism).
- Negligent retention. You hire a moron and either know it or find out he/she is a moron or worse, but you keep that person anyway. This usually is the fault of contracts that do not allow you to fire stupidity unless it falls into the extreme criminality with accompanying video.
- Negligent Entrustment. You allow a moron to have responsibility.
- Negligent supervision. No one was watching the moron.
- Failure to direct. No one told the moron what to do.

Chapter Eighteen

Stakeholders, Role Models, & Heroes

"I have ever deemed it more honorable and more profitable, too, to set a good example than follow a bad one."

-Thomas Jefferson

Stakeholder

There are over 470 synonyms for the term Stakeholder. I will use my own definition for our purpose here. A stakeholder is a person that has an interest in another person and can either affect or be affected by that person, sometimes without direct knowledge, association, or interaction. More often than not, the person that the stakeholder holds in high regard has no idea of his or her actual influence over that stakeholder.

I had that epiphany when I was a Patrol Lieutenant. I liked showing up at calls to see how my Officers were doing. I wasn't micromanaging. All leadership classes tell you to inspect what you expect. I expected to find good Officers doing their job, which I often did. On this occasion, I responded to a medical call, an apparent drug overdose. I walked into the kitchen of the home and found a young man, approximately in his late teens or early twenties, sitting on the floor leaning against the cabinet. He was obviously under the influence and not having a good day. As I approached him he raised his head up with glassy eyes and looked into my face and said, "Hey Officer Bob."

I hadn't been Officer Bob in many years, when I would give school safety programs as a Patrol Officer (before the D.A.R.E. program existed). I had apparently made some type of impression on this young man a decade or so ago, enough that he would remember me through his drug induced haze. I was impressed with this encounter, even though my message about "Just Say NO" may not have hit the mark. You never know what sticks with some people, good or bad. I was happy this individual, now in need of assistance, saw a friendly face in the crowd of Police and medical responders at a time when he could use one.

Earlier in my career, I arrested my share of people selling drugs. The local guys weren't evil, they just needed a better hobby. After one particular raid, I scooped up one guy for selling narcotics along with his mother and sister for jumping on me, to prevent me from arresting their son and brother. I think we dismissed the charges against the ladies but the dealer went to jail. I would see his mother from time to time on the street and ask how he was doing. When his time in the County Jail was up, he called me and asked me if he could use me for a job reference. I agreed as long as the job didn't have anything to do with drugs. I was glad to help him out. I felt I had a stake in his future.

For my class I always used the following example from the small, Rockwellian like town where I lived. Cranford had a population of approximately 22,000 people who were very proud of their school system. They also had a great sports program and often won State championships (girls as well as boys teams). Wrestling was among the favorite sports. The team had lost their wrestling coach and were in dire need of a replacement. The Board of Education conducted a search and found their prayers answered when they found Coach Dominic DiGioacchino. DiGioacchino, a 1976 NCAA champion, had been the head wrestling coach at East Stroudsburg University in Pennsylvania, but his contract had not been renewed in August of 1999 by ESU. The University cited insubordination as the reason DiGioacchino was let go. He took the coaching and teaching job at Cranford High School in that same year.[158] They held a meet the coach gathering with parents of the team and I found Coach Dom to be total dick. Instead of telling the parents how lucky he was to come to such a fine town and be given the privilege of coaching their children, he basically told us how great he was and we were the lucky ones to have him as a coach. The rest of the parents totally drank the Kool Aid.[159] I sat there dumbfounded at his audacity.

Just four years later, at 6 p.m. on Friday, April 11, 2003, Coach Dom was arrested in his driveway by the Union County High Tech Task Force. They seized his home computer and other evidence. The headline in the paper the next day read: Cranford coach held in cyber-sex attempt with Morris youth.[160] This is a headline every parent fears. My two sons had already graduated high school but it makes you wonder and ask embarrassingly uncomfortable and frightening questions.

The Union County edition of the Star Ledger had a follow up article on the following Tuesday, April 15th – Authorities say coach sent lurid emails, Cranford teacher free on cash bond. The Superintendent announced the coach would be suspended but had no further comment.[161] The Super never saw the OBPOS coming, and why would he?

The local paper ran the story in their weekly edition (below the crease) – Wrestling coach suspended after sex-related charges. The story tells of the three-month long investigation but still no further comment

---

[158] Mike Kuhns, *"Former ESU coach charged in N.J. sex case"* www. poconorecord. com, (April 16, 2003)

[159] On November 18, 1978, Jim Jones and more than 900 members of his People's Temple committed mass suicide in the jungle of Guyana by drinking cyanide laced Kool Aid.

[160] Jason Jett, "Cranford coach held in cyber-sex attempt with Morris youth" The Star Ledger, (April 12, 2003), N.P.

[161] Robert Missek & Jason Jett, *"Authorities say coach sent lurid emails"* The Star Ledger, (April 15, 2003), Pg. 33

from the Board of Ed.[162] On Monday, April 21, 2003, Coach Dom pled not guilty and remained free on $50,000 bail. The article expounded on the coach's credentials; former coach at ESU, ran summer wrestling camps at the University, national champion in the 177-pound weight division for the 1976 Division III squad at Montclair State University.[163] Disgustingly, the coach took no responsibility for his own actions as he deflected the charges by saying that he was distressed that he let his students down *by not being available to them the rest of the year*, not for being a sexual predator. He later changed his mind and pled guilty on August 28th to endangering the welfare of a child by photographing sexual activity.

Almost a year later, on Thursday, February 26, 2004, former coach Dom was sentenced to four months in jail. His wife of four years did not attend the sentencing.[164] On November 2, 2006, the New Jersey Department of Education State Board of Examiners formalized their decision to revoke coach Dom's Teacher of Health and Physical Education Certificate of Eligibility.

Coach Dom had an incredible negative impact on his numerous stakeholders. The local Board of Education went out on a limb for him and hired him with the expectation that he would obtain a teaching certificate and honorably represent their school system as a coach. The kids lost their coach, and to some, probably an important role model. The light of shame engulfed all the other coaches because the parents must have been thinking, are they safe? The coach's wife was also a teacher in another school district but the coach's story went state-wide. She knew all her fellow teachers knew her husband was a sexual predator. How does someone go to work every day carrying that with them?

---

[162] Steven Reilly, *"Wrestling coach suspended after sex-related charges"* The Cranford Eagle, (April 17, 2003), Pg. 1
[163] Judith Lucas, *"Coach pleads not guilty to obscene online talk"* The Star Ledger, (April 22, 2003), Pg. 19
[164] Judith Lucas, *"Ex-wrestling coach gets jail for e-mails"* The Star Ledger, (February 27, 2004), Pg. 35

Radio station NJ101.5 broadcast the case to over 1 million listeners who got to hear the shocking story as it unraveled. Daily radio shows cast aspersions over the entire town. The circle of impact grew wider every day. This is what I tried to convey to my recruits. What if it were you that did something illegal or maybe just embarrassingly stupid or improper. How would that effect your family, your friends, your neighbors, your co-workers? A bad situation usually lasts about five years. The coach disaster lasted 3 ½ years from arrest to revocation of his teaching credentials. He now is a registered sex offender and that doesn't go away. He had to forfeit his teaching, his coaching, his entire career with kids, including his summer wrestling camps. I have no personal knowledge of any lawsuits but they are a gift that keeps on taking. My question to my class is, "Would you take the same action if a member of your family (your mom) were standing next to at that moment you made the decision?"

*   *   *

Arthur Seale was an Officer with the Hillside Police Department from about 1970 to 1977 (my guess). He left the Force and went to work for Exxon in their security department. He and his wife Irene were living above their means at the time, so Artie came up with a brilliant plan to dig them out of the hole. It was not a brilliant plan. It was a terrible plan.

He decided that he and his bride would kidnap an Exxon executive and hold him hostage for the random amount of $18.5 million. His rational, in his own words were "the company would never miss the money and no one would get hurt…he and his wife never discussed the downside."[165] Einstein never thought going up against a global, multi-billion-dollar corporation and the Federal Bureau of Investigation may lead to a downside.

On April 19, 1992, the duo grabbed Sidney Reso in front of his home, accidentally shooting him in the arm. The brain trust shoved him in a van but forget to leave a ransom note. They stuffed the victim in a coffin like box and left him, wounded and without medical care or food and water. They left him in the sweltering box in a storage facility

---

[165]   Ted Sherman, *'Infamous N.J. killer seeks early release"* The Star Ledger, (July 18, 2020), Pg. 1

where he died four days later. They then buried him in the Pine Barrens. Two months later the pair was arrested.[166] Judge Garrett stated, "What you have done here is thoroughly evil." Arthur was sentenced to life in prison. His wife was released in 2010 after serving 17 years.[167]

There are two take-aways from this story. Number one is it doesn't matter how long you are or were a Police Officer. Going forward you will always be known as one. It doesn't matter if you quit the Department the day after you graduated from the academy (we had a guy quit the day before he graduated) or put in forty years of service, the media will refer to you as a former (or whatever tense) Police Officer.

The second point is the stakeholder side of the issue. A retired Hillside Police Officer that knew Seale's family told me, "His dad was a Deputy Chief and a nice guy and good friends with my dad. His mom worked in Hillside High School and was a secretary and was always helpful to the kids. His sister graduated high school with me. He (Arthur) did great harm, not only to the victim but also to his own family, including his children. Horrible incident, but Arti needs to stay in."

Arthur Seale now holds a PhD in consulting psychology and feels he should be released from prison (much of his time was spent in Supermax located in Minnesota) due to his age, health and ongoing pandemic.[168] Artie never thought about the downside of a sentence to life behind bars.

Carrie Maxwell Wrigley wrote, "I throw a pebble in the pond - Just a small one; But its ripples extend far and wide"

Role Models

John Madden[169] was interviewed by *Time* magazine in 2008 and was asked, "Do you think professional football players should be considered

[166] *"Couple arrested as Reso kidnappers"* The Star Ledger, (June 20, 1992), Pg. 1
[167] www.nytimes.com>1992/12/01
[168] *"Couple arrested as Reso kidnappers"* The Star Ledger, (June 20, 1992), Pg. 1
[169] John Earl Madden (born April 10, 1936) is an American former football coach and sportscaster. He won a Super Bowl as head coach of the Oakland Raiders, and after retiring from coaching became a well-known color commentator for NFL telecasts. Wikipedia.

role models?" His answer was his usual shy and subdued reflection, "Yes I do, and I think it ought to be written in their contracts. I don't think they have a right to say they are or they are not, because they are! And they ought to accept that!" I am sure he yelled this reply. I believe the same condition applies to Police Officers. Like it or not, you are a role model as soon as you accept the badge and you should be proud of it and enjoy being one.

In 1993 Nike's longtime advertising agency produced an honest, thought-provoking commercial that challenged social norms. Notoriously outspoken Phoenix Suns star Charles Barkley boldly and defiantly declared that he was not a role model and that kids should be taught to emulate their parents, not athletes or celebrities. "Just because I dunk a basketball doesn't mean I should raise your kids," Barkley concluded. Barkley took a lot of shit for that commercial.

"The first time I got hit really hard was for taking that stance," Barkley wrote in his 2002 memoir. "There were some columnists that defended me but mostly I got killed. I'm okay with it, though, because nobody in all this time has been able to convince me that it's wrong to tell kids to listen to their parents and not a basketball player they've never met." Among Barkley's most outspoken critics was a fellow elite power forward and alumnus of the Dream Team. In an essay entitled One Role Model to Another published in the June 14, 1993, issue of Sports Illustrated, Utah Jazz star Karl Malone wrote that being a role model was not Barkley's decision to make.[170] Charles Barkley was correct in that parents should be their children's first role models. Karl Malone was also correct in that Barkley had no say in who decides he is their role model. Police Officers, also do not have that choice. When I was Detective Sergeant, I kept a little figure of Lawrence Taylor on my desk because LT was friggin awesome. He was undoubtedly one of the best linebackers in the history of the game. Number 56 played with the Giants for 13 seasons from 1981 to 1993, was a 10-time Pro-Bowler and 8-time First-Team All-Pro, with 133

[170] Jeff Eisenberg, *"Iconic Sports Commercial: Charles Barkley's 'I am not a role model'"* Yahoo Sports, (July 17, 2019)

sacks (one that ended Joe Montana's career[171]). He was inducted into
Hall of Fame in 1999. Taylor's drug problem started around 1986 or at
least that was the first time he acknowledged it in public by entering a
rehab program. His issues continued throughout his career and followed
afterwards but he kept on playing like a monster. I finally put his figure
in my drawer when he stated that the Police (from several states) were
involved in a conspiracy against him. That is why he kept getting
arrested. It had nothing to do with the cocaine in his possession or
his personal criminal behavior. Congressman Dan Crenshaw put it
best saying, "People are flawed and imperfect, idolizing a particular
person as *the* person you want to emulate inevitably leads to eventual
disappointment or disenchantment It's tough losing a role model, even
when you're an adult."[172]

Taylor's record:

Nov. 18, 1985: Ends Joe Montana's career

Feb. 14, 1986: Enters six-week drug-rehab program in Houston,
stays one week.

March 20, 1986: Admits in public statement that he has received
help for substance abuse.

1987 Won Super Bowl XXI against Denver

Aug. 29, 1988: Given 30-day four-game suspension for second
violation of NFL's drug-abuse policy for cocaine use.

March 1989: Fails breath test when police find him asleep behind
the wheel of his Jeep beside the Garden State Parkway in N.J.

May 10, 1989: Acquitted in Saddlebrook, N.J., of drunken driving
charges

---

[171] Amber Lee, bleacherreport.com, (June 25, 2012) - Former NFL quarterback Joe
Theismann played his entire 11-year career in the NFL with the Redskins. The career
of the two-time Super Bowl winner came to an abrupt end during a Monday night
game Nov. 18, 1985 at RFK Stadium when Joe sustained a brutal break in both bones
of his lower right leg. The hit on Theismann came courtesy of Giants linebackers
Lawrence Taylor and Harry Carson—a going away present for a quarterback who
would never play again. Washington won the game 23 – 21.

[172] Dan Crenshaw, Fortitude American Resilience in the Era of Outrage (New York,
NY: Hachette Book Group, 2020), Pg. 37

1991 Won Super Bowl XXV against Buffalo

1993: End of career

Sept. 20, 1995: Tries to choke a reporter (I can see that happening)

April 16, 1996: Driver's license suspended for outstanding parking tickets in Newark, N.J.

May 3, 1996: One of 15 arrested in Myrtle Beach, S.C., for allegedly trying to buy $100 worth of crack from undercover police while in town for a celebrity golf tournament. Charges dropped when LT agrees to 60 hours of public service.

June 4, 1997: Pleaded guilty to filing false 1990 income-tax return and failing to report $48,000 income from the now-defunct LT Sports Club in East Rutherford, N.J.

May 13, 1998: Arrested in his New Jersey home in a roundup of deadbeat parents. Released after about 10 hours in jail when a friend pays $6,000 in child support and for an outstanding traffic violation.

Oct. 19, 1998: Arrested again, this time in Florida, for allegedly buying $50 in crack from an undercover cop and for possessing drug paraphernalia.

1999: Inducted into The Hall of Fame

Nov. 2009: Arrested in Miami for leaving the scene of an accident.

May 6, 2010: Arrested and accused of raping a teenage girl at a hotel in Suffern, N.Y. Every once in a while you get a real role model that does not disappoint. I am not a baseball fan and have no idea what half of the statistics mean but even I would have married Derek Jeter. *Jeter spent his entire 20-year MLB career with the New York Yankees. He was elected to the Baseball Hall of Fame in his first year of eligibility in 2020; he received 396 of 397 possible votes (99.75%)[173], the second-highest percentage in MLB history and the highest by a position player. A five-time World Series champion, Jeter is regarded as one of the primary contributors to the Yankees' success of the late 1990s and early 2000s for his hitting, base-running, fielding, and leadership. He is the Yankees' all-time career leader in hits (3,465), doubles (544), games played (2,747), stolen bases (358), times on base (4,716), plate appearances (12,602) and at bats (11,195).*

---

[173]   I want to know who the hell would vote against The Captain.

His accolades include 14 All-Star selections, five Gold Glove Awards, five Silver Slugger Awards, two Hank Aaron Awards, and a Roberto Clemente Award. Jeter was the 28th player to reach 3,000 hits and finished his career ranked sixth in MLB history in career hits and first among shortstops. In 2017, the Yankees retired his uniform number 2. They started spelling respect with Jeter's number because he was an all-around good guy, on and off the field. **R E 2 P E C T.** Nice! Derek Jeter was a guy you could look up to. Be a Jeter. The Army motto was Be All You Can Be for twenty years. The Police need to step up their advertising campaign and promote a new image as well as back it up with actions.

Heroes

It is easy to understand how role models are sometimes mistaken for heroes. That is because heroes can absolutely be role models but not all role models are heroes. A hero can be idealized for outstanding achievements but I believe the key ingredient to be a hero is selfless acts of courage. My first hero was astronaut, John Glen.[174] As an eight-year old boy, I watched in wonderment as the aluminum foil wrapped spaceman, climbed into, what I believed to be, a giant rocket and blasted off after a nerve-wracking count down. That was a true American hero. I knew right then and there I was going to be an astronaut. That was until I flew in a plane for the first time and couldn't handle it. On October 29, 1998, the first American to orbit the Earth made history again. John Glenn became the oldest man (77) to fly in space by serving as a payload specialist on STS-95 aboard the space shuttle Discovery.[175] I have heard others describe heroes as just regular people who face danger square in the eye, but don't back down. I have worked with heroes and have met many others. I have attended numerous 200

---

[174] **John H. Glenn, Jr.,** (born July 18, 1921, Cambridge, Ohio, U.S.—died December 8, 2016, Columbus, Ohio), the first U.S. astronaut to orbit Earth, completing three orbits in 1962 in Friendship 7. Later, United States Senator from Ohio In office December 24, 1974 – January 3, 1999.

[175] https://www.nasa.gov/centers/glenn/about/bios/shuttle_mission.html, (Oct. 29, 1998)

Club[176] affairs honoring the First Responder Heroes of that particular year in that County. In almost all of the incidents, the first responder jumped into an action that could have taken their own life. They had only mere seconds to move in the direction towards danger to save the life of another person; most likely a perfect stranger. As Yoda[177] said, "Do or do not, there is no try!"

Following the 9/11 attack on the World Trade Center in New York City, President George W. Bush addressed Congress[178] on September 20, 2001, just nine days after almost three thousand Americans were killed. It was an inspiring speech to unify the country and give us hope.

Great harm has been done to us. We have suffered great loss. And in our grief and anger we have found our mission and our moment. Freedom and fear are at war. The advance of human freedom the great achievement of our time, and the great hope of every time—now depends on us. Our nation—this generation—will lift a dark threat of violence from our people and our future. We will rally the world to this cause by our efforts, by our courage. We will not tire, we will not falter, and we will not fail.

It is my hope that in the months and years ahead, life will return almost to normal. We'll go back to our lives and routines, and that is good. Even grief recedes with time and grace. But our resolve must not pass. Each of us will remember what happened that day, and to whom it happened. We'll remember the moment the news came—where we were and what we were doing. Some will remember an image of a fire, or a story of rescue. Some will carry memories of a face and a voice gone forever.

---

[176] The 200 Club is a group of business people who support first responders by giving them the comfort of knowing that, if they pay the ultimate sacrifice for their service, they will provide assistance to the families, funding college scholarships for the fallen responder's children, and aiding in other ways.

[177] starwars.fandom.com/wiki/Yoda - Yoda, a Force-sensitive male being belonging to a mysterious species, was a legendary Jedi Master who witnessed the rise and fall of the Galactic Republic, followed by the rise of the Galactic Empire. Small in stature but revered for his wisdom and power, Yoda trained generations of Jedi, ultimately serving as the Grand Master of the Jedi Order.

[178] https://Legaldictionary.thefreedictionary.com/ George+W.+Bush%3a+Address+to+Congress%2c+September+20%2c+2001

And I will carry this: It is the police shield of a man named George Howard, who died at the World Trade Center trying to save others. It was given to me by his mom, Arlene, as a proud memorial to her son. This is my reminder of lives that ended, and a task that does not end.

President Bush was trying to tell us, the American people, not to be afraid. 343 firefighters perished that day along with 72 law enforcement officers during their rescue efforts that saved over 25,000 lives. President Bush wanted to give the nation a hero that they could believe in to fight against the evil that came into our country. He chose to hold up the badge of one of the Police Officers, George Howard, who had died as a powerful symbol that we still had Law and Order in a time of utter chaos. When it appears that the world is coming to an end, the Police will be there for you. I wish every new recruit and veteran could hear that speech today. I witnessed a hero in action right before my very eyes. I was one of two Lieutenants running patrol and we would alternate day and night shifts, with a slight overlap for communication. During that time, we would ride around checking on things and catching up on recent events. One afternoon we observed a large black smoke plume rising above a neighborhood. I drove towards it as my partner, Lt. John Sofie, radioed in that we had an active house fire. I pulled in front of an old Victorian house with flames shooting out the windows. I was about to pull up so I would not block the scene for arriving fire apparatus and Lt. John jumped out of the passenger seat and sprinted towards the house. I sat motionless for a few seconds, not believing what I was witnessing. He hit the closed antique front door full force, like Lawrence Taylor hit Joe Montana, and kept on going, as the door slammed shut behind him. I then gathered my senses and properly positioned the patrol car out of the way. I returned to the scene in a matter of seconds to see my partner coming back out the front door with an older woman draped over his shoulder. She had been unable to maneuver herself to safety. No one else had been home at the time. I submitted him for a lifesaving award, but like most things, internal politics got in the way and they denied him the award. One more things that sucks about law enforcement. Remember that cushy job in suburbia? Other Officers in my Department saved occupants from a vehicle fully engulfed in flames. On another occasion a cop crawled into an overturned car and held pressure on the victim's wound to stop the person from bleeding to death before the ambulance arrived. (No award) Another Officer worked his way up to a ground floor window where a sniper was taking pot shots with a bolt action rifle, firing .243 rounds next to elementary school. He pulled the shooter out the window and arrested the suspect without firing a shot. Before the sniper was captured, he had put several rounds into the responding police vehicles. (Once again no award) When I was a Patrol Officer, my entire shift responded to an early morning fire at a gas station that was directly adjacent to an old apartment building. Everyone put aside the thought of the entire gas station erupting in a fireball of an explosion but we knew we had to evacuate the apartment building quickly. We all ran through the building banging on doors and waking the residents, carrying out the children, and assisting the elderly to safety. It wasn't a choice. A smoky fire broke out in the Summit Senior Housing Complex. By a stroke of fate, sadly the entire Police Department was attending the funeral of one of the Officer's sons, who had been tragically killed in a motor vehicle accident. All members responded from the Church, which was literally across the street from the complex. All residents were rescued by the finest dressed response team ever, as everyone was in their dress blues for the funeral. Several Officers were treated at the hospital for smoke inhalation. It doesn't matter who you are or where you work. Someone, maybe a child, hopefully your own child or other family member, could be looking at you as role model or even their hero. They have something invested in you doing the right thing and maintaining that image. You may never know who that person is or what you mean to them right up to the moment they say, "Hey Officer Bob." It's your duty to work hard for that unknown person as well as all the others you do know, to uphold the highest standards of your Department and the person you are.

I am not one for polls because there are too many variables and credibility is always an issue but I will give you this information anyway to do with as you please.

A 2001 Harris Poll provided the following:

- They defined hero as a person distinguished by performance of extraordinarily brave or noble deeds
- Americans want even more - they want their heroes to persevere despite adversity, to go beyond expectations, to stay levelheaded in a crisis, and to risk themselves for the sake of a better society
- One half responding couldn't name a living public figure, politician, or athlete, they would consider a hero
- One in six had NO heroes
- One quarter had recently crossed someone off the list of heroes mostly because of unethical conduct
- Two thirds of those who lost respect for a hero said it was because the individual was overly concerned with their own personal recognition
- One third said their hero was a friend or relative (most often a parent)
- Nine of the top 20 American heroes are Presidents
- George W. Bush ranked 17th (probably due to 9/11)

But times change as do opinions. A 2016 Gallop poll found that a little more than ¾ Americans have a "great deal" of respect for the Police who patrol their communities. This was a significant uptick over 2015 and the highest since a Gallop poll in 1967.[179] Results of a new national poll in February 2020 showed support of local Police officers, according to an alliance of law enforcement officers. The United Coalition of Public Safety announced findings, saying that 82 percent of those surveyed believe that their local Officers are honest and trustworthy.[180] You do have to take into account the source of the poll, which was The United Coalition of Public Safety. Even so, look at where the Police stand now, according to most media reports! How far they have fallen in such a short period of time after the shit hit the fan.

---

[179] Mark Berman, "Poll: U.S. respect for police at highest level in half-century" Washington Post, (Oct. 26, 2016), n.p.
[180] *"National Poll Shows 82 Percent Favorable Opinion of Police Officers, A Law Enforcement Alliance Says"* https://losangeeles.cbslocal.com

Chapter Nineteen

The Backbone of Life

"If you want to support others you have to stay upright yourself."

-Peter Hoeg

The human spinal column consists of 33 individual interlocking vertebrae. Each one is vital to the entire structure. They work in conjunction with all the other vertebrae with three main functions;

1. They bear the load and allow you to move forward,
2. They protect the delicate spinal cord so you can continue to make decisions and function, and
3. They hold you together.

I have identified 13 crucial career factors that act as your life spine. Like your vertebrae, they are load-bearing, protect you, and hold you together. I leave you with 20 more free spaces, that you can name for yourself, to complete your own spinal column of life. These factors are independent of each other but depend heavily on the rest and take turns as the lead factor depending upon the circumstances of the moment.

At the start of my class I ask the recruits, "How long does it take to make a good Police Officer?" They, of course, are dwelling on their current painful and boring path through at least 20 weeks of screaming, running, and studying. Their answer is a logical, 20 weeks. I told them they were incorrect as, there is no amount of time, that you can make a good Police Officer. First you must start with a strong foundation of a good person and then mold them into a Police Officer. You don't take the Betty Crocker cake mix box and throw it in the oven and expect to pull out a ready-made chocolate cake. You need to gather the proper ingredients and follow the instructions. Here are the ingredients in no particular order of importance. Some of them you have control over and some you need to make the best of the situation, learn from it, grow, fight, and move forward.

Faith

In the 1991 movie, *City Slickers*[181], grizzled, hardcore cowboy, Curly (Jack Palance) explains to Mitch (Billy Crystal) what the secret of life is, "It's one thing, just one thing. You stick to that and everything else don't mean shit." Mitch asks what the one thing is and Curly tells him, "That's what you have to figure out."

The one thing is different for everyone. It could be religion (that works for a few billion people of all faiths) or anything else that makes you wake up in the morning, put your feet on the floor and face the day head on, no matter how crappy you may think it is going to be. It's the thing inside of us that keeps us going and gives our life purpose. It could be any of the things listed next, or it could be a specific thing only important to you. It's the strength you draw from when your inner tank is running on empty and you think you are done. It's that thing that pushes you beyond

---

[181] Wikipedia, *City Slickers* is a 1991 American western comedy film, directed by Ron Underwood and starring Billy Crystal, Daniel Stern, Bruno Kirby, and Jack Palance, with supporting roles by Patricia Wettig, Helen Slater, and Noble Willingham.

your limits, or keeps you from breaking down at your lowest point. It's that inner strength that you didn't know you had. It's the thing that drives you to do one more push up or run another 100 yards. It's the drive to do better, when you are about to say I guess that was good enough. Everyone needs to find their one thing because some day they will need it and it may save their life by pushing them through the impossible.

Family

You have to be 18 years old to become a Police Officer. Your family has most likely had custody of you for at least that long. Family could also be any mixture of individuals that cared for you; traditional mom and pop with possible siblings, two moms, two dads, an aunt Matilda and Uncle Fred, or just a Grandmama. Hopefully they did a good job with you but in the event they fucked you up, you still have a chance to become a better person and un-fuck yourself. Police Officers either come into the job with a young family or start a new one along the way. Your family experiences almost all of the stresses that are placed upon you. There has to be a fine-tuned relationship with all family members to prevent those stresses from tearing the family unit apart.

It is a common belief that the divorce rate for police officers is higher than that of the general population. This belief is commonly held in spite of the fact that there is no empirical research supporting such a belief. To compare the divorce rate of law enforcement personnel with the rates for other occupations, they analyzed data from the 2000 U.S. Census. Surprisingly, the results of this analysis indicate that the divorce rate for law enforcement personnel is lower than that of the general population, even after controlling for demographic and other job-related variables.[182]

The family has to understand the requirements placed on you and be able to give you the support to meet those challenges. Missing family

---

[182]   McCoy, S.P., Aamodt, M.G. *"A Comparison of Law Enforcement Divorce Rates with Those of Other Occupations." J Police Crim Psych* **25,** 1–16 (2010). https://doi. org/10.1007/s11896-009-9057-8

activities is one of the most difficult side effects of the job. You cannot be in two places at the same time, and often you don't get to choose your preference as duty calls. You also have to remember that your family carries the cop label. Just as I have said, you can be branded if your asshole kid does something bad (even if you have already retired), your family is, the spouse or child, of a cop. You can't erase any of your mistakes. You have to live up to the badge for them as much as for yourself. It is a two-way support system and it requires a tremendous amount of work to hold it together and remain strong.

Friends

I covered friends briefly in an earlier segment but they are another critical part of your overall well-being. You should not have only friends from your specific field of work (this applies to any field of work). Can you imagine a room full of accountants at a party? That sounds like more fun than a barrel of moneys. Even a barrel of monkeys would invite a warthog to the party to add some spice. You require different points of views to keep you sane. You need to hear arguments from an opposing side. When everyone always agrees with you all the time and you are surrounded by yes men and women, you wither and die. A perfect example is the numerous entertainers that had their hand-picked entourage with them wherever they traveled, but no one strong enough in the group to stop them from doing drugs, that ultimately led to their untimely and early death. That said, you need to dump the losers you grew up with. Maturity and common sense are not passed along to everyone. When you enter your twenties, you need to have a bit more responsible attitude. It's time to put on your big girl or pants.

Co-workers

You may pick up your first co-worker friends in the Academy. I believe the unwritten rule in the Academy I instruct at is, "don't even think about getting caught in a strip joint." No good shall come of this. If you have time to watch boobs, you have time to study, work out, or shine your boots. In 2014, nine probationary Port Authority of New York and New Jersey Police Officers lost their jobs because of a rowdy graduation party (that means they had already completed the entire Academy). The Agency investigated reports that Officers were drunk and out of control at a Hoboken bar following the August graduation of the 113th class.[183] The Hoboken Police responded first and immediately identified One Big Pile of Shit and called the Port Authority to deal with their own mess. They wanted no part of it. The recruits had gone through and completed all that work and spent all that time for nothing. The powers that be figured the recruits weren't going to improve much from there so they cut their losses. The bosses knew the Department was throwing away thousands of training dollars but the decision to fire the entire bunch was made in the best interest of the future of the Department. As Spock always said, "The needs of the many outweigh the needs of the few." He was Vulcan right.

Start making the right decisions at the very beginning. Some of your co-workers will become your lifelong friends. You will save each other's lives and hopefully keep each other out of trouble. This does not mean you will cover for their mistakes or make excuses for them. That will just land you back in OBPOS. Then you both lose your jobs. You should work to make each other better. Some of your co-workers will become closer than family. I have been fighting with my old partner for over forty years. I wouldn't have it any other way.

Physical Condition

I have already stated that the Academy is the last time you may be in top shape (or any type of shape for that matter). Loss of muscle mass, also known as Sarcopenia, occurs as a result of aging. After age 35 you will lose between .5 -1% of your muscle mass annually unless you engage in regular physical activity to prevent it. By engaging in regular

---

[183]   newyork.cbslocal.com, "Rowdy Graduation Party at Hoboken Bar Costs 9 Port Authority Police Officer's Their Jobs"

resistance training and following a sound diet that includes adequate amounts of protein, you can prevent most of the muscle loss associated with age. Health experts recommend that you engage in some type of resistance training that focuses on all major muscle groups a minimum of 2 times per week and up to 5 times per week depending upon your goals.[184] Staying alive is a very good goal.

You will promise yourself that you will work out and stay in shape but you are a delusional lying sack of dog shit. It is not going to happen. You're lucky if you have the time to play with your toddler. The above deterioration rate is for an average person. Police are not average people. Police are highly more self-destructive. This rate is accelerated with the addition of sleep deprivation (shift work) and maximum stress (every day) mixed with driving around in an uncomfortable vehicle for inordinate periods of time. Supplement this formula with tobacco and/or alcohol and you have the perfect cocktail for early death. Are we happy yet? No one is going to hold your hand and lead you to the gym. No one is going to give you a time out for not doing your sit ups, and you will not get a cookie if you do.

The fun part begins when you strap on an additional 30 pounds of equipment around your waist that disrupts your center of gravity and exerts undue pressure upon your lower back. Now sit on an overstuffed leather wallet for eight to ten hours and you give birth to herniated discs and painful crippling sciatica (put the wallet, and your stupid phone, in your shirt pocket). Besides the three useless tools (spray, baton, gun) they provide for you to use for your defense and now prosecution, the only real things you have to defend yourself is your mind, strength and skills. How much can you count on yourself when backup is an excruciating five-minutes out, and you are rolling around on the ground, all alone, with a sweaty, alcohol or drug infused suspect, who is twice your size? This is a scenario that should give you pause. You should not be too busy taking care of everyone else that you forget to take care of yourself. Remember the flight attendant speeches – put on your oxygen mask first or you won't be able to help anyone else. Smart folks, those flight attendants.

---

[184]   National Academy of Sports Medicine. sharecare.com

Appearance

Appearance goes hand-in-hand with physical conditioning. If you work out properly, you should look good. I want to smack the people at the gym who bring reading material or phones to the workout. Put that shit down, work out, and get the fuck out. I've seen guys sitting on a bench at a machine reading, totally monopolizing the equipment. Do they work out in the library?

You will never know everything but if you look the part you can get by in a lot of situations. When the New Jersey State Troopers are not racing a caravan of high-end luxury cars down the road at break neck speeds (sorry I couldn't resist), they look very professional and are the perfect image of authority. They always look sharp. If you show up looking that good, people just expect that you know what the hell you are doing. The other part of that is, don't show up with lunch all over your tie.

I have to include an example from my own Department. One Officer was a good guy, smart, very friendly, and strong as a bull. Problem was he was a total unmade bed. He looked like he had slept in his locker. He had one shirt with a tear in it so he wore a raincoat over it, ON A SUNNY DAY! I blame the supervisor for allowing him to get away with it. When this Officer showed up on a call, no one took him seriously and would often challenge him. The Officer would always win the struggle but why bother if you don't have to exert yourself?

Austin Kleon[185] said, "You have to dress for the job you want, not the job you have, and keep dressing to keep it." I had a great Sergeant who was an obsessive neat freak. He would scrub the engine of his personal 57 Chevy Belaire with a toothbrush. His uniform was always meticulously clean and perfectly ironed. At that time we carried Smith & Wesson .357 revolvers. A single row of highly polished silver bullets adorned his black leather gun belt (ala The Lone Ranger). These rounds

---

[185] Austin Kleon became a web designer for the law school at University of Texas. Kleon published his poems as Newspaper Blackout. After Kleon's first book was published, he became a copywriter for Spring box, a digital ad agency. Kleon's work has been translated into over a dozen languages and featured on major media.

were supposed to serve as reloads if a situation arose when he needed it. I had the chance to ask him about these rounds one day and he told me, "Oh they are just for show." I do not endorse carrying extra bullets for show because each round counts, especially when you carry a revolver, but he was an example of what professionalism looked like. Squared away, I believe is the term used in this instance.

Education

My favorite saying is, you don't know what you don't know. As a matter of fact, the more I learn, the more I know I don't know. Law enforcement requires that you be the smartest person in the room. You have a great advantage when you know more than the other people at a scene. This is beneficial when dealing with homeless crack addicts to millionaire business moguls. The motto from Farber College in the movie *Animal House* was Knowledge is Good. Francis Bacon[186] said, "Knowledge is power." Both of these statements are correct. When you have the knowledge, you are not easily fooled and can see down to the root of the issue or problem. Your knowledge will allow you to come up with a reasonable solution.

You do need to know everything. First off, you need to know the laws, to make sure you are covering all your bases before you react. I can guarantee that you will be challenged, and challenged often (mostly during a vehicle stop and of course in Court). You need to know your Department's Rules & Regulations to make sure you are following procedures their way. You need to know what your contract says to make sure you are covered for doing the right thing. What are you entitled to? What happens when you fuck up? (And you will.) You need to know local ordinances and motor vehicle law. You need to know

---

[186] Wikipedia, Francis Bacon was an English philosopher and statesman who served as <u>Attorney General</u> and as <u>Lord Chancellor</u> of <u>England</u>. His works are credited with developing the <u>scientific method</u> and remained influential through the <u>scientific revolution</u>.

the players in your town, including the Mayor and Council, as well as their kids. Not for special treatment, but for your own self-preservation.

You need to know everything about drugs and weapons for your own survival and testimony in court. Lawyers take great pride and amusement in trying to make you look like a fool. One time, I was sequestered from my partner on a drug case. He went into the courtroom to testify first. It gave me time to do some calculations. When it was my turn, I took the stand and the lawyer started with his standard routine questions. "So how long have you been a Police Officer," he began. I answered, "Approximately five years." He jumped at that answer and repeated it back to me as if I were a moron. "Approximately?" he mocked with his shit eating lawyer grin. I came back at him with my hallway calculation, "Four years, 10 months, 23 days" and then I looked at my watch, "and four hours!" The stenographer stopped typing and looked up from her machine and gave me a thumbs up. The lawyer backed off immediately. We won the case.

Never stop learning. Take advantage of every opportunity, especially if it's for free. If your town pays for college, GO. Keep going. Learning is like working out. You have to put forth an effort to make the time for it but it also pays off at the end. Read every report. Read every law enforcement bulletin, because shit changes on a daily basis. What was correct yesterday will land you in jail or fired tomorrow. You can never learn too much. And just like your outside friends, have a diverse library that you are drawing from. Read newspapers (especially the local rag so you are aware of the issues and problem areas and issues in town), magazines, and as many books on all topics that you can devour. Well-rounded is your goal.

I had a conversation with a Secret Service Agent (while we were on a protection detail for Marilyn Quayle[187]). He told me that his Agency required ANY college degree. It could be in Art. The Secret Service was looking for someone older than 18 years old, which a degree gets

---

[187]   Wikipedia, Marilyn Tucker Quayle (born July 29, 1949) is an American lawyer and novelist. She is the wife of the 44th vice president of the United States, Dan Quayle, and served as the second lady of the United States from 1989 until 1993. Her protection detail hated her because she would run long distance at 5am every day.

around any age discrimination, and someone with some life experience. The trend is swinging back in that direction now.

Some New Jersey Police Departments have had college requirements since the 1990s. Most agencies including the NJSP, ask for either a bachelor's degree or a combination of military experience.[188] To make this a uniform requirement, they will need to change the entire Civil Service testing procedure. Christopher Wagner of the New Jersey Association of Chiefs of Police stated, "Just because you went to college doesn't mean you're going to be a better police officer, but an honorable, professional, ethical Officer who is also college educated would make a better, well-rounded Police Officer."[189] If they made college a requirement like other professions, the applicant would bear the cost of schooling and remove that expense from the tax payers.[190] A college requirement also opens up a myriad of other obstacles. That is for others to figure out.

Training

Professional training is an extension of your physical training. I told you that your department will only train you ENOUGH to meet the minimal standards for liability purposes. Does anyone really think firing a deadly weapon two hours a year meets any type of proficiency standards? In the U.S. the average training academy is 21 weeks (840 hours) according to a 2013 Bureau of Justice Statistics report. After the academy the recruit is then assigned to a training officer for a period determined by the respective hiring department. In some European countries training can last more than two years.[191] Germany requires

---

[188] Rebecca Everett, *"Educated cops use less force, research shows"* The Star Ledger, (June 30, 2020), Pg. 1

[189] Ibid

[190] John Vespucci, *"College grads make for better police officers"* The Star Ledger, (Aug 23, 2020), Pg. A6

[191] Rebecca Everett, *"Educated cops use less force, research shows"* The Star Ledger, (June 30, 2020), Pg. 1

30 months, Ireland, two years, while Finland and Norway requires a three-year police college.[192]

Think about musicians, athletes, dancers, any professionals, or any type of instructor (yoga, karate, Zumba). They spend hundreds maybe thousands of hours a year to prefect their skills. To put this in perspective, a Cosmetologist License requires up to a minimum 1200 hours (over 300 hours more than the Police Academy).[193] Cops spend two hours of mandated training a year at the range with an instrument that can take a life. This makes no sense at all. A cello player laughs at how little police practice. That training, my friend, is on you. You not only have to make the time but may also have to put out your own cash, as bullets are not cheap. This also applies to your baton and any other equipment including handcuffs, that you carry. If you don't use it, you lose it. The old joke goes; How do you get to Carnegie Hall?[194] Practice, practice, practice. Every cello players knows this. Every day is Game Day, be ready.

Mental Attitude

Now, more than ever, Police Officers need to maintain a calm and controlled demeanor. This is easier said than done. There are a plethora of social media videos showing protesters taunting Officers, not more than mere inches from their face. This is another skillset that needs a great deal of practice. You can start off-duty with yoga or similar relaxation techniques. You have to be at one with yourself. You must be in control at all times. Keep all exterior sounds out and treat it as if it were white noise like rainfall. After a strenuous call is over, take a minute by yourself to calm down and let the adrenaline rush pass. You

---

[192]   John Vespucci, *"College grads make for better police officers"* The Star Ledger, (Aug 23, 2020), Pg. A6

[193]   Ibid

[194]   Wikipedia, Carnegie Hall was built by philanthropist <u>Andrew Carnegie</u> in 1891 in New York City, it is one of the most prestigious venues in the world for both classical music and popular music.

need to return your body functions like respiration and heart rate back to a normal level.

When you are first given a call from dispatch, you will automatically react in accordance to the tone of the dispatcher. If they are excited, you get excited. There have been studies that show just activating the lights and siren can drastically increase your heart rate. You have to be aware of that. Your response time is the time you are not only being hyper alert to any traffic hazards, but also the time you are preparing for your arrival at the scene. What will be your approach? What happens if you get there first? I would guess that most Officers forget that they can back their vehicle up after they initially stop if they need to reposition more safely or determine there is imminent danger at that exact location.

You need to be mentally ready when you arrive for your shift. You need to store all your personal baggage in the overhead compartment (or your locker). In marriage they say never go to bed angry. In law enforcement you can never go to work angry or upset or worried, or tired (good luck with the last one). You need to be able to think clearly. Emotions may taint your decision-making process or the words coming out of your mouth. Control is the key to success and a safer shift.

I had arrested this mildly disturbed person for creating some type of ruckus. He did not resist and the arrest was under control. He was handcuffed and I led him back to my patrol unit to transport him to headquarters for processing. Just as I placed him in the back seat he stated, "Your momma sucks African cock." This statement took me off guard and then he continued, "Okay you can beat me now."

I turned to the individual, whom I had never met before, and asked, "Do you feel better now?" He stated he did and so we skipped his expected beating as there was no need for it. He had been upset about something, and he needed to get his emotional outburst out of the way. We were both satisfied we weren't required to undergo any physical encounter, because it wasn't worth it.

The best in-service class I attended was Verbal Judo. It is the art of turning one's opponent's words against them as in actual Judo, deflecting the attacker's blows. The best line from that class (I tell my class to write this shit down - WTSD) was, "Say what you want as long as you do what I say." Let the bad guy call you anything that makes them happy. As long as they are following your directions then you won. A perfect example of this is how wives use this on their husbands. They tell you to throw the trash in the middle of an NFL playoff game. Your natural reaction is to start grumbling. She (the wife) does not hear a single word that you are saying as you get up and throw out the trash. Who won?

Confidence Level

When you combine all the previous points, it builds your confidence level to an acceptable working comfort zone. This level arrives at different times depending upon the individual and their specific learning curve. At some point, in any job, you say to yourself, "I got this." You should never get too sure of yourself where you get cocky. Cocky gets you killed. Never be complacent because you think you have everything under control. Most times you never will have everything under control. You always need to improve no matter how good you think you are because you're not that good. Someone is always better. I gave my Sergeants an evaluation to fill out on me as their Lieutenant expecting glory and accolades from the heavens, and possibly a parade. They fucking killed me. It served as a good reality check for me and made me work harder to get better. You don't know what you don't know. Sometimes you have to ask, even if you don't like the answers. Sometimes the truth hurts and sometimes it is helpful.

Supervisors

I mentioned that the bad guys are often the least of your worries. There is a thing referred to as the *Toxic Boss Syndrome*. The phrase is used to describe a circumstance where the man or woman in charge is so arrogant, hostile, and entitled that coming to work can actually be a traumatic experience for subordinates (I hate the word subordinate) - even for Police Officers.[195] These bosses suck the energy out of the individuals in their groups. They are belittling, petty, and loud. They consider themselves better than everyone else, and they don't care who knows it. They are certainly not Superior Officers. All they care about is getting the job done their way (maybe not the best, fastest, or correct way). They care mostly about themselves. In their drive to achieve their goal they ignore, overlook, or demean the other people in the organization. And in the end, it helps no one.[196] I can honestly say I should have earned an honorary degree in dealing with toxic bosses. I can fill another book with stories from law enforcement and corporate experiences.

I once had a supervisor who was so arrogant it would be embarrassing to be in his presence. An F.B.I. Agent arrived at my Department to assist me in a bank robbery investigation. As protocol the Agent professionally identified himself with his proper title. He stated, Hello, I am Special Agent so & so." My boss responded in his usual rude fashion, "What's so special about you?" in the most condescending tone he could muster. That served absolutely no purpose and kicked off the investigation on the wrong foot. The man was a human stress factory. There are hazards of the job as in all professions, but toxic bosses are the silent killer that you can't change, and sometimes just have to endure the pain and wait for them to either retire or die. I would go so far as to schedule my vacation at a different period from a bad line supervisor's vacation so I could extend my time away from him. Toxic bosses can make or break you. The one positive thing they do for you is make you stronger if you don't let them get to you first. The old saying is if it doesn't kill you then it gives you ulcers.

I wasn't going to include this next short story in fear that you would mistake me for a whiney bitch complaining about being picked on. Then I remembered the words of Tom Cruise in the movie *Risky Business* when he said, "Sometimes you gotta say, what the fuck." So, here is my boohoo, woe is me story, as my perfect example of a Toxic Boss.

---

[195] Apbweb.com/toxic-boss, American Police Beat
[196] F. John Reh, *"How to deal with toxic boss syndrome in the workplace"* (March 31, 2019) thebalancecareers.com

All the Officers, with the rank of Sergeant and above, were seated in a conference room waiting for the Chief (because he is the only person who can be late) to start the staff meeting. He burst through the door like Kramer arriving in Jerry's apartment on the Seinfeld show. He immediately turned to me and started a red faced, profanity filled, spit flying tirade, asking me who the fuck I was for changing policy and blah blah blah.

The Deputy Chief had asked me to enter some information in the day book which was used for patrol at daily briefings to update them on the latest developments. I followed these instructions as he was my direct supervisor. The Chief continued dressing me down in front of all the other supervisors in the room as the Deputy Chief sat silent. I was used to this treatment and had entered my Zen zone. I showed no emotion or other physical concern as the shouting continued. I didn't even glance in the direction of the person who had thrown me under the bus and who was now allowing it to back up for another pass at me.

I do not know if the Deputy Chief ever came clean and fessed up to the Chief that it was him who directed me to make the specific entry in the book. I never heard another word about it and never received an apology from either person. That is pure toxicity.

There are good supervisors and bad supervisors everywhere. I have had my share of both. Learn from them all about what to do and what not to do. Everyone you meet, good or bad, knows something that you don't. The most important lesson is to praise in public but punish in private, not like my staff meeting encounter. Cherish the good bosses as they are few and far between. Practice being in your Zen moment when you are with the bad ones. If you show them that they got to you, they win. When you become a boss, remember how you wanted to be treated and don't be an asshole.

Working Conditions

Law enforcement as a whole fell in love with the Post World War II decorating theme to the extent that it embraced the entire design concept. For the longest time, most Departments could double as a set from a Humphry Bogart movie. That continued until some Departments were able to get federal funding to construct cold cinder block boxes (similar to prisons) to call home, complete with the old 1950's furniture from the previous building. Grants were only for the structure. If Departments were really lucky, a local company would allow them to take away their outdated furniture to use. We were like the Salvation Army Police begging for handouts.

I actually began my career in a south Jersey municipality as a dispatcher. It was very similar to working for the Dukes of Hazard. We wore almost the same uniforms as the Hazard County Sheriff's Department. The entire Department was stuffed into a bomb shelter type basement of what they considered the Municipal Building. The good news was, that it was the 70's so there was money available to build a new Police Department.

The bad news was that we (members of the Department) would come in, on our day off, and literally BUILD the new Police Department, for free (that means we didn't get paid to do it). Contracts? We didn't need no stinking contracts. I did learn how to hang sheetrock from the experience. Thank goodness the grant that funded my position ran out, and they laid me off.

I was hired by my second and last Department a year later and took up residence in a 100-year old converted school building. The asbestos would sprinkle down on us from the ceiling when we slammed our lockers shut. On one occasion a pretty blue flame shot out of the wall switch when I turned the hallway lights on. The black scorch mark remained on the wall until we moved out of the building. The report room was too small for two people. I brought in one guy on a warrant who was over 7 feet tall. All you could see were these giant legs sticking out of the room as I typed up his arrest report.

We had the old-fashioned Police desk that sat up high so you had to look up at the Desk Officer when you entered the room. Everything was paneled (so it didn't have to be painted or cleaned). The only protection (rumor had it) was a metal plate imbedded inside the wall of the front of the desk in case someone came in shooting. There were no protective barriers, security cameras, bullet-proof glass, or reinforced doors so an attacker only had to shoot over or around the desk, if they were so inclined.

The arrest/drunk driving testing room was also the break room so we ate off the same surface on which all the toxic contraband was placed. If someone was brought in during a meal break, everyone had to leave and go eat on the staircase. As bad as our lunch room was it was still better than the Detective break room, which was a windowless 6x6ft. square. When I was in the DB, at least seven grown men (excluding me) managed to squeeze themselves into the room and chain smoke cigarettes. The single tiny wall vent fan hardly sucked any smoke out of the room, but if it did, it sent the smoke into the main Detective Bureau area. It was cancer central.

As bad as this sounds, this was luxury accommodations compared to some other Departments I had visited. When I served with the Auto Theft Task Force, we spent a majority of our time in Newark, because that's where all the stolen cars ended up. Some of their precincts were dreadful. We had to bring our own typewriters with us because they either didn't have any that worked or there were no spares. The bathrooms were usually out of order and smelled like the Bronx Zoo The overall condition of the entire building was horrendous, bordering on condemnation.

Getting back to my favorite cushy suburban Police Department comment; these guys in the inner city worked their asses off, got paid less, and worked in literal shit conditions. Life is not fair. To find a ray of sunshine in this mess, a Patrol Officer's office is the patrol vehicle. They would spend the major portion of their day driving around unless they were required to come in and do paperwork (and there is always a shit ton of paperwork to do but computers have changed that – many reports can now be completed in the vehicle).

Law enforcement sits at the bottom of the totem pole in priority and it clearly shows. The only reason my Department moved into a brandy new building was (1) The old building couldn't meet any State regulation standards, and (2) They changed the original plan from a new Police Department to a new Municipal Complex (which turned out to be too small for the Police Department on day one – go figure). Lesson to be learned – keep your vehicle as clean as it will make you happy.

Financial Status

I have previously mentioned that Police Officers turn into overtime whores. Why? Because they can. Shift work allows you the freedom to work additional hours for a decent rate. Way back in the Bronze Age, we received $25 for three hours work (before taxes). Now total amounts that Officers bring home are front page news and hot political topics. If the overtime is caused by a manpower shortage then that is the choice of the Municipality, not the blame of the Officer who signed up to cover a shift. The Municipality chooses not to hire more Officers to save on additional costs like benefits. Then they play stupid when they are called on it and don't explain the breakdown and cost analysis to the public. The newspapers like to play it up like Officers can go work whenever they want and take home, boatloads of cash for free (have I mentioned I hate reporters?).

The trap to avoid is getting hooked on the O.T. It is a fine line from working some overtime to working too much. Some Departments are implementing time period limits that Officers have to go home and get some rest. I had a few very fine Officers who starting fucking up because they were not thinking clearly. Simple things like, forgetting to place the vehicle in park before getting out to write someone a ticket, causing the patrol vehicle to crash into the car that was going to receive a ticket. It does catch up with you.

And then there is the abuse. It starts getting easy to sign up for jobs and either short change the time spent at the particular location or not show up at all. Many Officers from many Departments have succumbed to this trap. Since there is a paper trail, it often leads to numerous problems and resulting punishments including dismissal and criminal charges.

And the winner for The Stupid Overtime Award goes to Jersey City Police Department. Although, many other Departments have fallen prey to the same bad decisions, Jersey City was so bad that they went above and beyond just stupid to the point that they started a Federal corruption probe focusing on off-duty, private security work. By the end of 2016 they had already ensnared one Officer and expected to arrest at least a dozen more.[197]

Jersey City Officers were permitted to work off-duty, providing security for private companies, which at that time was supposed to go through the City, so, that the City would get their cut of the action, (referred to as administrative fee – totaling in the hundreds of thousands of dollars). The City collected their piece similar to a Mafia Vig[198] that amounted to $12/hr. on top of what the company paid out to the Officer. The investigators targeted Officers who cut the City out as the middleman (shorting the City out of a huge windfall of cash) and either performed the work under the table or took the money without working.[199] In an episode of the Sopranos, the guys joked about the problems of their no-show jobs. They didn't know what not to wear to work or what not to bring for lunch.

This off-duty work was as if the Golden Goose and the Cash Cow gave birth to a Leprechaun. Officers could have made between $35 and $65 an hour. In one year one Officer made $129,445 above his annual salary of $121,338. (I apologize for falling into the media game of stating salaries except these people did it wrong). The records showed Officers received a total of $14,892,946 between January 1st and November 17th in 2016 for off-duty jobs. It was no surprise the guy in charge of distributing off-duty jobs to Officers fell first.[200]

By January of 2017, they had placed a dozen cops on modified duty and taken their weapons away. The City spokesperson did not release

---

[197] Terrence T. McDonald, *"Feds' probe targets cops, sources say"* The Star Ledger, (Dec. 28, 2016), Pg. 15

[198] Urban Dictionary - The Vig is the interest to a <u>loan</u> on the street or through a <u>bookie</u>. It is common to not <u>pay back</u> the principle but have to pay the "<u>vig</u>" or interest weekly to keep your legs intact. The interest paid in no way lowers the principle.

[199] Terrence T. McDonald, *"Feds' probe targets cops, sources say"* The Star Ledger, (Dec. 28, 2016), Pg. 15

[200] Ibid

the names of the Officers but, of course, "a source with knowledge of the investigation" (another scumbag who also should have been fired) did. One Officer had already pled guilty to one count of conspiracy to commit fraud and accepting corrupt payments and one count of filing a false tax return (that's how they got Al Capone).[201]

As July rolled around, five Officers had pled guilty and faced up to five years in prison and repayment of money they had received illegally. They also faced disciplinary action and of course termination (because it is difficult to be a cop when you are in prison).[202]

The new year (2018) didn't start off any better as the Chief, a 38-year veteran of the Department, admitted in court to charging up to $31,700 from the Jersey City Housing Authority for work not performed. He faced a maximum penalty of ten years in prison and a potential $250,000 fine. He was the tenth Officer to plead guilty.[203] At least two years into the investigation, the Mayor finally decided it would be a good idea to end the off-duty program, with no plan on how to fill the need for off-duty Officers.[204] (And that's how politicians operate – they have no idea where they are going but they are making good time.)

Because life is not fair, the ex-Chief, the guy in charge and the person that is supposed to set an example for the rest of the Department, received one of the lightest sentences among the other 11 ex-Officers in the now rotten barrel. He got two-years- probation (six-months of home confinement), and paid a $10,000 fine. The real zinger was that a Judge ordered the 63-year-old ex-Chief to retain only benefits on money he contributed to his pension, but the State would no longer contribute its portion.[205] (ouch)

---

[201] Terrence T. McDonald, *"12 cops put on limited duty amid feds' probe"* The Star Ledger/The Jersey Journal, (Jan. 11, 2017), Pg. 17

[202] Terrence T. McDonald, *"3 more cops face prison in federal probe of Jersey City"* The Star Ledger/The Jersey Journal, (July 26, 2017), Pg. 3

[203] Terrence T. McDonald, *"Ex-Jersey City cop chief admits stealing $32K"* The Star Ledger/The Jersey Journal, (Jan. 5, 2018), Pg. 4

[204] Terrence T. McDonald, *"Fulop vows end to jobs program for off-duty cops"* The Star Ledger/The Jersey Journal, (Feb. 2, 2018), Pg. 13

[205] Michelangelo Conte, *"Judge revokes ex-police chief's pension, benefits"* The Star Ledger/The Jersey Journal, (Aug. 11, 2019), Pg. A19

Here were a dozen guys with various amounts of time on the job, including the Chief with almost four decades, that couldn't see they were headed straight for One Big Pile of Shit, because they had become overtime whores. This is a deadly trap that ensnares even some good guys. "Greed is a bottomless pit which exhausts the person in an endless effort to satisfy the need without ever reaching satisfaction.[206]

I had the unfortunate assignment of running off duty jobs (different from shift overtime in which Officers worked for other agencies, like Board of Education for sports events or utilities for traffic control). This was the worst job I ever had but tried to do it to the best of my ability (legally), and I did not get arrested. It sometimes would take hours to fill a slot. This procedure changed several times because no one was ever happy with the way it worked. I knew I had a fish on the hook when an Officer was getting married. Marriage means a lot of bills that require a lot of money that requires a lot of side work or overtime shift work. I wasn't overly cruel. When an Officer came to me to request time off to get married, I would sit them down and explain that if they wanted me to, I could deny their request and get them out of the wedding and they could blame the whole thing on me. No one took me up on it. Don't laugh, the New Jersey State Troopers used to have to ask permission to get married.

Don't become an overtime whore. Stay within your budget. Enjoy the time with your family. Listen to Cat Stevens'[207] (now Yusuf Islam) song, Cat's In the Cradle. Time is precious, don't waste it.

---

[206] Erich Fromm

[207] Wikipedia, Yusuf Islam (born Steven Demetre Georgiou; 21 July 1948), commonly known by his stage name Cat Stevens, and later Yusuf, is a British singer-songwriter and multi-instrumentalist.[1] His musical style consists of folk, pop, rock, and, in his later career, Islamic music. He was inducted into the Rock and Roll Hall of Fame in 2014.

Chapter Twenty

Haters Gonna Hate

"Darkness cannot drive out darkness: only light can do that.
Hate cannot drive out hate: only love can do that."

-Dr. Martin Luther King Jr.

Hating the police now rivals baseball as America's new pastime. I'm sure there are some out there who are actually keeping their own score cards on their favorite Police Department teams. I have already told you the reasons why people hate the Police but let us recap in case you weren't paying attention.

1. Police are authoritarian figures, and no one likes to be told what to do. In the 1960s, the Police were a mere extension of government suppression. They were The Man, pigs, gestapo, storm troopers, and everything else that represented evil. We watched the Police beat civil rights marchers, college kids and the "law-abiding people" at the 1968 Democratic National

Convention in Chicago. The Vietnam War didn't help the Police image back here in America.

2. Just seeing the Police makes people crazy and uncomfortable. In the 1970 album Déjà vu by Crosby, Stills, Nash, and Young, David Crosby wrote *Almost Cut My Hair*, which turned out to be the hippie generation anthem. James Perone wrote that the line from that song, "It increases my paranoia/like looking into a mirror and seeing a Police car," more than any other song of the entire era, captured the extent of the divisiveness in American society regarding violence and terror.[208] We thought things were bad then, but now are ten times worse. Everyone reacts when they see a marked police car. Who doesn't look down at their speedometer, often too late?

3. Police are thugs, bullies, and murderers.
1991 – Rodney King was beaten by several LA Sheriff's Officers.
1999 – NJ State Police accused of racial profiling
1997 – Abner Louima was violated by the NYPD with a broomstick (very unpleasant circumstances).
1999 – Amadou Diallo was tragically shot and killed by four NYPD plainclothes officers.
2012 – Trayvon Martin was shot by a civilian that had nothing to do with the police (the 911 operator told the shooter, George Zimmerman to stop following Martin) but people think the police killed Martin.
2014 – Michael Brown was killed by an Officer who was defending his life but that is not how it is remembered
2020 – George Floyd, allegedly suffocated by Minneapolis Officers lead to national rioting and demonstrations.

---

[208] *Perone, James E. (2012),* <u>The Album: A Guide to Pop Music's Most Provocative, Influential, and Important Creations, Volume 1</u>, *The Praeger Singer-Songwriter Collection, ABC-CLIO, p. 21,* <u>ISBN</u> <u>9780313379062</u>.

4. Everyone knows how to do the job of law enforcement better than the people hired to do it. The public has been watching Police shows and movies since Thomas Edison invented the kinetoscope.[209] Everyone has turned into an expert Monday morning quarterback with perfect 20/20 hindsight to review the plays. They (including the attorneys, prosecutors, and juries) all now enjoy all the extra time to analyze the three or four seconds that the Officer had to make his or her life and death decision. The O.J. Simpson trial lasted almost 8 months.[210]

    The average Joe on the street now qualifies as a Doctor of Jurisprudence (especially teenagers and teenagers of real lawyers) and they know their rights, which means they think they can do anything they please. They are mistaken but they believe they are always right. This creates resistance, which eventually leads to trouble for someone and now that means for the Police Officer, no matter who was right to begin with.

5. Police make too much money. (It's all about the Benjamins) Police Officer's salaries have improved drastically and especially in the Northeastern United States (also a higher standard of living = taxes). Police make more than an average person as well as receive a lifelong pension if they are lucky enough to retire and live long enough to enjoy it. I have discussed overtime and working after retirement. Neither of these legal options are acceptable to the public.

---

[209] www.britannica.com, Kinetoscope, forerunner of the motion-picture film projector, invented by Thomas A. Edison and William Dickson of the United States in 1891. In it, a strip of film was passed rapidly between a lens and an electric light bulb while the viewer peered through a peephole.

[210] cases.laws.com/oj-simpson-trial, The OJ Simpson Trial was a criminal trial that occurred in 1994; both the hearing – as well as the deliberation of the OJ Simpson Trial lasted for upwards of 8 months. The OJ Simpson Trial is not only considered to be amongst the most prolific, but also the longest within the history of the United States. The glove didn't fit so they had to acquit.

6. Everything is the fault of the Police.

    Over the years law enforcement has become the dumping ground for problems, many of which cannot be solved by them. Things like homelessness, poverty, mental illness, domestic violence, drugs, gangs, illegal immigration, traffic, failing infrastructure, high taxes, and myriad of other things that cannot be handled by one agency, and especially one with great restrictions, while at the same time working under a microscope.

7. Many people believe that dying is part of the job of law enforcement.

    This can't be farther from the truth. Police Officers are not supposed to die doing their job. They are supposed to live to help other do the same. Dying is a tragic consequence that occurs after an incident has gone horribly wrong. This is one of a few select occupations where others actively seek to end your life.

    General George Patton expressed this thought during his address to the U.S. 6th Armored Division on May 31, 1944, "No bastard ever won a war by dying for his country. He won it by making the other poor dumb bastard die for his country." Although the Police are not the military, they are the closest thing to an occupying force in this country that sees battle every day. It is the same concept. Officers are not supposed to die in the line of duty but they all too frequently do. We lose on an average, about 112-120 law enforcement Officers per year or one Officer somewhere in the country every three days.

    I have attended too many, in the line of duty, Police funerals. It is today's Viking funeral minus the flaming arrows and the boat. They are very impressive with all the fanfare of bag pipes, gun salute, and always the saddest version of taps played on a trumpet. The more horrible the circumstances of the death, the bigger the attendance of uniformed Officers dressed in their first-class attire, sometimes numbering into the thousands.

I show news clippings of the most recent funeral to my class and ask them, who wouldn't want this as a going away party? Before they have a chance to answer, so I don't have to embarrass them, I yell, "No one!" This is not your end game plan. If anyone gets killed after graduation, I'm going to kick their ass! I do not allow this type of mindset in my class. If you want to be a hero, then be a hero, but live to tell about it.

The Police are not the innocent party here either in the hate game. It takes two to tango[211]. The Police hate the public equally. Sure, they started the job expecting to be the caped crusader, zooming onto the scene and fixing all problems or solving a crime in the allotted 60 minutes of a TV episode. They all wanted to be that masked man that rode off into the sunset leaving a grateful group of well-wishers behind. Fat chance bucko. I received more thank-yous and praise working the door at a funeral parlor than I ever did in almost three decades in law enforcement. Let that sink in for a while. I literally only opened a door for a grieving family as compared to saving a life with CPR or pulling someone out of a car wreck. My advice to future Police Officers is don't expect anything and you won't be disappointed. You do the best job you can, every day and be satisfied with that. So, here is why the police hate everyone:

1. See all of the reasons I have already presented.
    Police get the blame for everything, even when many of the policies have been passed down to them by the know it all politicians. One New Jersey Governor saw that Police wrote a lot of expired registration summonses. What could this mean? More cash for the State. They jacked the price of summonses from about $25 to $175 (not including court costs if you contest it). They did the same for not producing proper documents (license, registration, insurance card). A simple violation could add up in significant fines. Police used to write an inspection

---

211   Both parties involved in a situation or argument are responsible for it.

summons as a "gimme" ticket." That was giving a motorist a break for a more serious offense. Inspection was a cheap non-point summons. Everyone walked away, maybe not happy, but satisfied that it was a fair outcome (that is the definition of a compromise). Police thought the drastic increase in the fine was outrageous and unfair so they stopped writing the ticket. The public never knew the Police were fighting for them.

2.   People defy the Police.
     Police only expect people to obey the law and do as they are told. That's it! That plan has not worked out since assholes, Adam and Eve, violated the first rule of the planet. Officers are given the role as the parent to tell the kids to do or not do something that would keep them safe (it's for their own good). It's like the rule: don't touch the stove. Sometimes you only have to tell someone that once. Everyone chooses which rules they will follow and are surprised and shocked when they are singled out for an infraction. They, the public, feel they are being picked on (harassed) because they are a certain gender, race, religion, have a certain hair style, are wearing a hat, or because (my favorite) the police had nothing better to do with their time. Not because the driver just blew a red light. Most common responses heard - I stopped officer or as Elwood Blues said, "The light was yellow sir!" When they asked for my name for MY horrible behavior, I would tell them I would make sure to write in clearly on the bottom of the ticket so they could read it.
           Many simple arrests turn tragic because the person being arrested thought that it would be a good time to resist the Police or pull a weapon. (Remember my hunting knife wielding speeder?) Do these people think they are going to escape forever by fighting the Police? There are a lot more out there to come and get you.

3.   The stupidity index is through the roof and the Police have zero tolerance.

This is another category that could fill another book.[212] Let me provide just a few examples. There was a terrible accident that required the response of a great deal of emergency apparatus. I had the entire street blocked with several marked Police units, the entire Fire Department with all their big red shiny trucks, a couple of ambulances, and at least one large tow truck. A driver slowed down and stopped facing the scene. As I walked up to her she stated, "I have to go this way." I stepped aside and said, "Go ahead." She then realized I was an asshole and turned around. Most people do not understand the simple concept of – go around the block. They have lived at their home for numerous years but only know one way to get there.

Another – I am in the process of arresting someone, actually handcuffing the individual. I have the suspect leaning against a vehicle and someone approaches me to ask directions. I wanted to unhandcuff the person I was arresting and place them on the person asking directions.

One more. I'm standing on a corner in a busy section of the downtown and a young mother walks up and stops with a small child in a stroller. The front of the stroller was sticking out into the intersection as she stood safely on the curb. Because I am/was an asshole I had to speak up, I asked her if she didn't like this one that much? (I certainly would not last long in today's world on the street.)

4. People teach their children to hate the Police.
A parent walked into headquarters with a small child in tow. They pointed to the Police Officer and said, "this man is going to put you in jail if you don't eat your vegetables." The old-time Lieutenant responded, "that's right, teach the kid to hate and fear us so when he gets lost, he runs from us instead of looking

---

[212] Here is a shameless plug for another one of my books – *Just Plain Stupid* covers all categories of stupid.

for our help." (There were many of us that would not last a day in this new age of entitlement and self-righteousness.)

5. At one point there was a website called RateMyCop.com. The creators of the site gathered Officer's names, which was public information, from over 450 Police Agencies. They said the site would help people rate more than 130,000 Officers by rating them on authority, fairness, and satisfaction.[213] Of course this brilliant idea was covered by the 1st Amendment.[214] What could possibly go wrong with an anonymous posting of opinions after an interaction with the Police? The site can no longer be reached.

6. The real reason cops hate everyone is that they mostly see the worst in people on a daily basis. Sure, there are good people and many support the Police, but they are the ones that mind their own business and follow the rules. There is a reason that cops get cycled out of assignments like vice and narcotics, because it can be very taxing on any human being. The temptation is also very high to get enticed into that lifestyle because you have to live it to get close to the bad element. Could you imagine working child abuse cases for any length of time? That shit will rip a person apart.

7. There are close to another thousand reasons why Police hate everyone with the changing political climate but that is for someone else to figure out. Let us suffice it to say that the tide has turned drastically against the entire policing concept and it doesn't look like it will get better any time soon. In the words

[213] CBS13 Correspondent R.E. Graswich has the scoop on how police are reacting to sites like RateMyCop.com

[214] Constitution of the United States, Congress shall make no law respecting an establishment of religion, or prohibiting the free exercise thereof; or abridging the freedom of speech, or of the press; or the right of the people peaceably to assemble, and to petition the Government for a redress of grievances. (1789)

of Sgt. Phil Esterhaus from *Hill Street Blues*, "Let's be careful out there."[215]

I conduct a few exercises with my class, time permitting, and it never did. This one I call Heart Surgeons and Trash Collectors. I handed out two small pieces of paper to each recruit. I then instructed them to rate their own ethical behavior from one to ten, ten being the highest. In the twenty years I have instructed the class the results have always turned out the same. I draw a 1 to 10 scale on an easel and then check off every response. The grouping usually falls from 7 to 10. There is always one moron that writes a number 1. Either they were too stupid to understand a 1 to 10 scale or are not ethical enough to be in the class. They probably shouldn't be in the class anyway if they couldn't figure out a one to ten scale.

I then have them do the same thing and write down a number representing society's ethical standing. The range drops drastically. This shows that the recruits believe they are better than the average person. I believe that this would work the same for any group polled including heart surgeons and trash collectors. The reason for this is that most people believe they are good people, their occupation has nothing to do with it.

I leave this question with the recruits. How would you rate if this poll were given to the general public? They all agree they would fall closer to the far lower side of the scale. You need to understand the reality of your surroundings. You may think you are the best thing since sliced bread,[216] but you aren't worth shit in the eyes of some of the people you are responding to or trying to help. Your first problem out of the gate when you get to the scene is, how come you took so long to get there? He had a hat!

---

[215] Hill Street Blues was a favorite cop tv series that ran from 1881 to 1987.
[216] Wikipedia, Sliced bread is a loaf of bread that has been sliced with a machine and packaged for convenience. It was first sold in 1928, advertised as "the greatest forward step in the baking industry since bread was wrapped".

Chapter Twenty-One

Changes

"I smile at obstacles."

-Tiger Woods

Like it or not, the job changes you. All jobs change you in some manner but Law Enforcement gives you that little forever something special. If you are fortunate enough to retire and not become an alcoholic or substance abuser and not be divorced at least once, you will at least get some consolation prizes to take home with you.

One of the biggest changes you will experience is pain.

Every job creates various stress on a person's body from carpet installers who have bad knees to office workers who develop carpal tunnel from hour after hour at a keyboard. There are many different classifications of pain, but I am not in the medical profession so I'm not going to try and explain it to you. You will recognize your specific pain when it finds you, and it will find you as there is no place to hide from it. All I can tell you from personal experience is that pain hurts. Chronic pain is the gift that keeps on giving. I, myself, wake up every morning at least a #4 on the zero to ten pain scale. This is now my life. I am never that smiley face on the physician's wall chart.

For Law Enforcement personnel, pain is usually brought on by years of abuse to your entire body. I always compare Police Officers to professional football players, except without the padding, the enormous paycheck, and adoring fans. Both professions have a given shelf-life with a floating *"Use by Date"*, like a carton of milk. Members of both professions have, on average, disregarding a catastrophic injury (Joe Montana), about ten good playing years. After that, they continue to rapidly deteriorate both physically and mentally from all the hits.

I have always said that the pain starts at 30 years of age and there is no going back. If you already have pain, cheer up, it will get worse. I know this to be true because I cheered up and it got worse. Every stupid thing you have ever done in the past will come back with a vengeance and at the most inopportune moment. You may be walking down the street and an unseen lightning bolt will catch you just right, zap. You have to turn around and look to make sure someone didn't sneak up on you with an electric cattle prod. Moving forward, you will get new pain from carrying over 30 lbs. of equipment incorrectly on your hip, for the life of your career. This will literally destroy your lower spine, and I have the pictures (x-rays) to prove it. The remainder of your joints will follow suit as the rest of your body attempts to compensate for the initial damage and tries to correct itself. It will not correct itself.

And then there is the time-consuming, life-sucking "routine patrol". The human body has survived millions of years of evolution but was not built to endure eight, ten, or more hours sitting in a Chrysler with a modified police package. Car manufacturers are finally catching up on ergonomics but for most, it is too little too late. The fact that most Officers reach the height of their physical peak while they are attending the training academy doesn't help the situation. The fitness graph after the recruit graduates can be captured in a steady downward slide like a graph of the 1929 stock market. I tell my recruits that most of them will turn into a fat piece of shit in the not too distant future. If you have gone to college, then you have experienced the freshman fifteen. Same concept. Patrol pounds!

A full-time job does not grant the luxury of time for young Officers to maintain a strict physical fitness regimen. Shift work complicates this matrix exponentially. When you get home, the last thing you want to do is put your body under more physical demands. You are more likely to reach for a Budweiser than a dumbbell. The general public also has no idea how boring "routine patrol" can be. The classic explanation is that Police Work is 59 minutes of excruciating boredom followed by one minute of extreme terror. You have to keep yourself amused during the 59 minutes so what do you do? You eat. Comedian, Jerry Seinfeld refers to this time alone with yourself as an unsupervised eating environment. You are often alone, but a partner is of no help to you to curb your snacking. The partner may be worse than you are and drag you down with them. Usually the first conversation of the day after the daily briefing is, "What do you want to eat for lunch?" You are a grown up now (at least physically) and no one is there to say, "You can't eat that." In fact, you not only can eat garbage your mommy told you not to, you can eat as much of it as you want, whenever you want. This is one of Dante's levels of hell. Your aorta will pay you back for this abuse in time. One of my "robust" Officers told me he was in shape because a circle is a shape. You can't argue with geometric logic.

Eyesight

Your retinas will burn up from staring at computer screens. Now mobile data terminals (MDTs) are standard installations with most patrol vehicles. Looking at your stupid phone all the rest of the time doesn't help. One more reason to dump the phone. You should require glasses by the age of 40. I first learned of my visual deterioration when I was riding with a young State Trooper assigned to the Auto Theft Task Force. He was driving and he asked me to grab a license plate of vehicle ahead of us to check it for stolen. I not only could not read the plate of the car down the block. I couldn't see the car.

OCD – Obsessive Compulsive disorder

If you have it already it will get worse. You will start checking things over and over for no apparent reason. I still check that my alarm clock is set at least three times every night even if I don't have to get up early. Sometimes I go around the block to see if I closed my garage door (it is always closed). OCD works to your advantage some times because it makes you more thorough. Like, is your gun loaded? Check, check, check. Once, I responded to a shootout without my weapon and it was a very uncomfortable feeling. The expression is - being as useless as tits on a bull. I never did that again.

Officers are not at all self-conscious about this disorder. They are proud to tell you in great detail of their specific routines. One guy told me that when he arrived home at the end of the day, he took all the loose change out of his pocket and had to place all the coins face up. No reason. Another fellow weighed himself every day at a local pharmacy. He would write his weight in his notepad along with what he was wearing at the time. He remained approximately 165 lbs. for 25 years. Once again, I am not a medical professional, and I do not know the root cause for this OCD phenomenon. It is classified as a mental disorder, but I believe everyone has something. There is no real "Normal". The goal is to have less disorders than others.

I have not seen cop OCD to be debilitating in the Officers I have known or worked with. No one I know was ever trapped in their house turning on a light switch 500 times. I think the OCD gave us all an order to things. Officers need to be in control even when things are out of control. Their OCD provides them structure, something to hold onto. I quote Rudyard Kipling:

If you can keep your head when all about you
Are losing theirs and blaming it on you,
If you can trust yourself when all men doubt you,
But make allowance for their doubting too;
If you can wait and not be tired by waiting,
Or being lied about, don't deal in lies,

Or being hated, don't give way to hating,
And yet don't look too good, nor talk too wise.

You Become More Tactical

Some may call this paranoia but I prefer the term hypervigilant. There are not a lot of jobs where people intentionally attempt to kill you. The acknowledgment of this possibility does not end when you take off the uniform. This vigilance needs to stay with you 24/7/365. In fact, it never goes away, not even with retirement. The old joke goes, "Just because you are paranoid, does not mean they are not after you."

You start watching everyone all the time, especially in public and at events. Active shooters are everywhere. At movies, at the gym, and the worst places are restaurants. (Aren't all mob guys wacked while they were eating linguini and clam sauce?) You need to sit facing the door, always. The significant others of Officers know exactly where they should sit in a restaurant without being directed to do so. My son and daughter-in-law were also cops and it was awkward when we all went out to dinner. The three of us wanted to sit on one side of the table with my wife on the other side. My wife was not pleased nor amused.

When having a conversation with someone you will look passed them and focus on others in the background. You can hear the words the other person is saying to you. You don't need to see them. Sometimes it comes off as being rude or inattentive. It is the opposite. You are fully aware of the situation and are being vigilant in keeping the both of you alive.

You tend to stand with your back to a wall or support column in malls and similar surroundings. You can never allow anyone to surprise you from the rear. You absolutely hate surprise parties. This was demonstrated in one of the Police Academy movies when the surprised birthday boy opened fire on the guests when he walked in the room and they yelled surprise.

You tend to keep track of where everyone is in the room. It could be a gym or small store. You need to know why they are moving in the direction they are moving and what they are going to do when they get there. You also need to read every license plate in your head in case you have to be hypnotized at a later time to recall the number.

Tactical Driving

When driving your personal vehicle, you will get suspicious of anyone driving behind you who makes more than two turns with you. I was coming home from a late shift one night and noticed a car behind me. I turned into my neighborhood and it turned with me. Now he has my attention. I made another turn and the car followed me. This is a quiet neighborhood and not a cut through street. I came up to the side of my house and passed it by as the car behind me slowed and stopped across from MY house. The driver turned off the lights as I drove on. I went around the block and turned off my lights and eased up behind the now parked vehicle. I silently exited my truck and approached the vehicle. I noticed the driver's window open so I quickly stuck my gun in the driver's ear to get his attention. I nicely asked the driver what he was doing. He stuttered back that he thought his wife was having an affair. I didn't know him or where he thought his wife was. I told him I didn't care and advised him he needed to go home. I believe he needed to go home anyway to change his pants. Hey, can you blame me? (I also tell my recruits not to follow my example.)

You also don't allow anyone to drive adjacent to your vehicle. You either back off or speed up. You don't drive parallel with anyone. That's a no-no. When driving down a main street you will always shoot a glance down each side street you pass, just because. I drive my wife crazy when I am the passenger. We would pass a side street and I would say, good on this side. She didn't understand (you won't either unless you have driven like a maniac in pursuit).

Once again, boredom is dangerous. We would test each other's tactical driving skills when working. When we drove past each other on patrol, we would toss a banana in either the driver's window or passenger window, if it was open. It passed the time and kept us sharp. We were tactically alert for fruit.

PTSD Post-Traumatic Stress Disorder

PTSD is another mental health disorder that arises due to previous exposure to a traumatic, dangerous, scary or shocking event - Isn't that why you took the job?
Symptoms:

1. Isolation from others, emotional numbness
2. Disturbed sleep, flashbacks, nightmares,
3. Increased irritability, extreme anger, depression
4. Decreased interest in significant activities
5. Self-destructive or reckless behavior

I called this Thursday. Let's break these symptoms down.

1. Isolation from others – After you're with cops, you don't want to be with Not-cops. Most Not-cops are not fun and they don't have your back. Cops are usually up for anything. Not-Cops are not. I have already told you Not-Cops do not understand The Fish Story. Years after Law Enforcement I ran for municipal office. At a very nice backyard fundraiser (comes with the territory), this apparently alcohol-fueled guest, wanted to engage me in a fight for reasons of his own making. I looked around and saw that I was in the company of Not-Cops, that were also suburban, pastel-colored sock golfers. I knew I was on my own had the situation escalated to the point of fisticuffs. My wife on the other hand was ready to jump in, which would have gotten me hurt, while trying to protect her. She finally understood my directions to walk ahead of me should the idiot try to ambush me from behind as I walked to my car at the end of the evening.

2. Disturbed sleep – This is another one of those presents that keeps on giving. After decades of sleep deprivation and round the clock shift work, your internal body clock is a total mess. They say that even a broken clock is correct twice a day. Your

clock however, is fucked. You don't know whether to eat breakfast or dinner. Combine that with the tanker truck of caffeine you drink on a daily basis and a horrible diet and you may never regain a normal schedule again. In addition to the time warp, you will see and do shit that is so crazy, horrible, absurd, or terrifying that it doesn't go away. It may pop up at any time. It may take a while to surface but it will come to visit. I enjoy waking up every night at around three. That seems to be a good time to think. It may not be all bad shit, but it will be enough to wake you up. This is another good reason to talk with other cops about the stuff you can't or shouldn't talk about with your spouse. You need to flush out your system.

3. Increased irritability – And why not. You deal mostly with the worst element of society or regular people on possibly the worst day of their life. There are very few instances you are called to respond to a birthday party to help blow out the candles. You work, what seems like all the time, in every kind of weather, miss special occasions, eat bad food, wear uncomfortable clothes, and get yelled at by almost everyone. Who would expect you to be in a good mood? Retired cops want one thing, to be left alone. They are done with people.

4. Decreased interest in significant activities – This is a misstatement. It's not that we cannot have fun doing normal stuff, it is just that doing crazy shit is so much better. We can absolutely appreciate a wedding or a little league game but smashing through a door not knowing what is on the other side trumps ordinary. I had the opportunity to be the ram guy during drug raids with the Narcotics Task Force. I was given a large, wide metal pipe with a flat plate on one end and handles on the side. It was my job to hit the door and knock it open during a raid. I had my own personal lunatic behind me as the shotgun man. He had my back and should a bad guy be

standing on the other side of the door when it swung open, the lunatic would handle it. It was amazing.

5. Self-destructive or reckless behavior – Hello, this is part of the job description. Carry a deadly weapon and make people do things they absolutely do not want to do, like get arrested. When assigned to the Auto Theft Task Force, I would often leave for work in the middle of the night to muster at our headquarters at Newark Airport. On the way there I would say to myself, "I'm going to die, I'm going to die, I can't wait to get there, I can't wait to get there." This was a time before there were hard core rules regarding car chases. In essence, we made it up as we went along. Most of our procedures were later banned in the New Jersey Vehicular Pursuit Policy of 1985. Boy did we have fun. The adrenaline rush during a high-speed pursuit in an unmarked car is indescribable. It was like the French Connection every day. The chase often ended in a crash and subsequent foot chase. On one memorable night, I was riding shotgun and involved in yet another chase. We were no more than inches from the suspect vehicle's rear bumper and my partner started to laugh. I said, "What the hell are you laughing at?" He gave me an answer I was not expecting nor did I care to hear. He said, "This is going to be a hell of a wreck!" We survived. Reckless behavior, oh yeah!

6. Stress will also manifests in other ways like IBS, ulcers, rashes, chest pains, nausea, dizziness, frequent colds or flues (because stress weakens your immune system), migraines, and of course the lovely pain that I have already covered.

You will have a better understanding and respect for death than most people.

I worked for a small suburban City so we only experienced seven murders over the course of my career. Chicago calls that a good weekend. The good news for us was that all our murders were all domestic violence related and were cleared quickly with either the arrest or death of the significant other. We could honestly say that you had a 100% chance of being killed by someone who loved you, right up to the point that they didn't.

We had our fill of a variety of other deaths, because people die. There were motor vehicle crashes, fires, household accidents, health issues, and a plethora of imaginative suicides. I remember one case where I believed we had an honest to God mob hit because we found a man strangled in his bed. I was young and naïve and had never heard of the term, autoerotic asphyxiation. The man had hung himself trying to get his jollies.

Probably the worst accident that turned into a suicide was when a young girl fled from a mental health facility and leaped onto the roof of an electric train car that was stopped at the below grade station. To the horror of the commuters, she burst into flames and amazingly lived long enough to get to the hospital after receiving enough voltage through her body to run a train. Pigeons would often attempt to land on the high voltage wires and explode on impact emitting an unbelievable sound.

It doesn't matter if you live in the same town that you work in or not. Eventually you will respond to the death of someone you know. One tough call was a standard medical response to a possible heart attack. I immediately started CPR. My Sergeant arrived a few seconds after I did. I then learned that the gentleman on the floor who I was trying to breathe life back into was my Sergeant's father. My Sergeant stood behind me consoling his mother as they watched. The Medic Unit was on the way but I knew it was hopeless. I didn't stop CPR, but continued to put on a good show as we always did for the family, to give them peace that we had done everything that could be done. He didn't make it.

I performed CPR along with another Officer a few years later on another older man. We were successful on that occasion. In a terrible twist of ironic fate, I returned to the same household about a year later when the son of our CPR save had committed suicide. We had saved the father, only for him to see the death of his son. The son had shot himself with a small caliber pistol.

The point of this story was the cause of death. I was the Detective assigned because I had responded to the scene and was obligated to attend the autopsy. I watched as the Medical Examiner removed the young man's brain from his skull. She then meticulously sliced it open revealing the pathway of the bullet across the man's brain. The bullet had traveled a straight line from the entry point at the right temple and stopped just before exiting the other side of his head, leaving a slight bump, visible from the outside.

I was amazed that an object slightly larger than a garden pea could end a person's life, efficiently and instantly. I had seen many dead bodies up to this point but this "show & tell" moment was an eye opener. It brought home the fragility of human life. I gained new respect for life and death.

You will develop one hell of a sick sense of humor.

This isn't to be mean or rude to anyone, it is to cope with situations presented to you. It also assists you in dealing with the absolute absurdity of the occupation. Death is a common occurrence; sometime you come across more than one body in a day. I, myself, have never scored a hat trick[217] in this category. When attending autopsies one would note the weights of the organs removed from the unfortunate guest of honor, after they were inspected by the Medical Examiner. The Officer would then purchase corresponding lottery tickets to match the numbers provided. It kept your mind off the fact that you were spending time with a person that was being cut apart shortly after they had their last bad day.

The crazy and/or homeless people (I know, not politically correct) kept us amused as long as they weren't trying to hurt anyone including

---

[217] www.nhl.com A **hat trick** as **hockey** fans know it comes when a player scores three goals in a game, usually earning him a cascade of **hats** thrown onto the ice by fans (especially if the player is on the home team). A natural **hat trick** is when a player scores three consecutive goals in a game.

themselves. I know that sounds harsh but the cops were the only people that really cared about them, looked after them, gave them money for food, or even took the time to talk to them. We also knew their names. No one else did.

It was the people who were not at a disadvantage that we made fun of and got a kick out of their misery often brought on by themselves. I was in charge of the Traffic Bureau, and a woman called one morning to complain that people were violating the two-hour parking regulation in front of her house. I told her I would take care of that for her and directed the district car to enforce the parking on the street. The same woman called me back later that day and told me she received a summons in front of her house. The conversation went like this:

Her – "I called you before to tell you about the people parking in front of my house"

Me – "Yes ma'am"

Her – "I asked that you enforce the two-hour parking regulation"

Me – "Yes ma'am and I told you I would take care of it"

Her – "There is an officer outside right now writing parking tickets"

Me – "Yes ma'am"

Long pause

Her – "I got a ticket. What am I an asshole?

Me – silence (but smirking uncontrollably)

Her – "Thank you" slams the phone down.

Sometimes it doesn't get better than that. There were thousands of incidents like this. Best part of the job.

And then there is the suicide thing.

More Officers die of suicide every year than die from shooting and traffic accidents combined. Andy O'Hara writes, based upon his 24 years of experience on the job, I believe that work-related stress and depression are far more prevalent in Police Work than reports suggest. Law enforcement is one of the most toxic, caustic career fields in the world. While injuries like PTSD are increasingly acknowledged within the military, its prevalence in civilian Police work goes virtually unnoticed.[218] Fortunately, there are more resources today like the organization Cop 2 Cop. COP 2 COP is a free and confidential 24-hour telephone Help Line. It is available exclusively for law enforcement Officers and their families to help deal with personal or job-related stress and behavioral healthcare issues. In 2019, 228 current or former Officers died by suicide, compared with 172 in 2018.[219] What kind of organization allows their employees to deteriorate to the point that they rob banks, kill others, or themselves? Law enforcement needs to take better care of their own. Starting at day one.

I have lost two friends, one former and one active Police Officers to suicide. The first one had left my Department before I had joined to pursue his own business. He remained in touch with the Department as he had many friends still on the job. I was fortunate enough to get to know him through them. He had also stayed active in our Police Athletic League functions.

I responded to an emergency medical call early one Sunday morning. The report was of an older male in distress in a vehicle. I arrived and found a van parked in the driveway of the home. There was a male in the driver's seat. I opened the door and found it to be my friend. He was unresponsive and apparently been there overnight. I found a wound to the center of his chest and located his revolver on the floor of the van. He was one of the nicest people you would want to meet and of course the family did not see this coming. My Chief responded to the scene minutes after I did. He had been best friends and neighbors with this

---

[218] The Marshal Project, (Oct. 3, 2017), Sgt. Andy O'Hara spent 24 years as a California Highway Patrol Officer (CHPs). He is the founder of _Badge of Life_, a nonprofit that offers police suicide statistics, training and program resources to ensure good mental health and prevention of police suicides.

[219] Luke Barr, _"Record number of US police officers died by suicide in 2019, advocacy group says"_ abcnews.go.com, (Jan 2, 2020)

gentleman for decades and had worked alongside of him. It was horrible in many ways for everyone.

The second Officer was an active member of the Department in my home town. He was also part of a Police Family. His suicide occurred after a lengthy period working during a weather disaster. Again, the family never saw it coming. The entire Police Department was devastated. The goal of this course was to eliminate some of the factors that may lead to Police Officer suicide. Avoid that One Big Pile of Shit, avoid getting into that situation, avoid the additional stress of facing Departmental or criminal charges, trial, sentencing, termination, jail, loss of career, reputation and family.

Chapter Twenty-two

Moving Forward

"Prior Proper Planning Prevents Piss Poor Performance."

-British Army adage

Have I mentioned that law enforcement hates change? Well it does, but everyone in it, or that has anything to do with it, knows that the entire Criminal Justice System needs an enema to clean it out from top to bottom. Winston Churchill once said, "Democracy is the worst form of government except for all those other forms." The same principal holds true for the American Criminal Justice System. It is drastically overwhelmed, excruciatingly slow, and not really a true "justice" system. All of the judicial and penal system shortcomings are blamed on law enforcement because cops act as the doormen to the entry level of this sometimes, never ending, revolving door to hell.

Right now, they are doing the best with what they have, but there is an intrinsic belief or fear that we can't do any better or we can't back out of the procedures that have been long established but are no longer working. It's kind of like President Johnson's refusal to get out of Viet Nam because he felt it would make America look bad. This thinking helps no one and hurts many. If anyone has ever worked for any business or agency, they are bound to come across a totally stupid procedure, if you ask why they do it that way, the answer is because that's the way it has always been done. That answer may be as moronic as the procedure that continues to be followed. You may even get the mom and dad answer, because I said so. Equally dumb answer. Parents know this is stupid when they are saying it.

You don't change for the sake of change. That only aggravates everyone more. I believe we have enough data to determine a better course of action right now. I will give you a perfect non-law enforcement example. If you have ever tried to change a reservation for an airline flight, you will find the process to be lengthy, ridiculous and often overly costly for no other reason than they make it so. All the person at the counter or on the phone has to do is type in the change. They tell you this is impossible. I have found that when someone tells me something cannot be done, it absolutely can be done, and often with less time and effort than it takes them to deny the request. I have succeeded in several projects through my policy of "progress through aggravation". If you are persistent enough, then you will persevere. If you are rude or act like an asshole then you will be excommunicated from the process or punched in the face. You need to have patience and stay calm. Remember this if you are ever on the other side of the issue and in control if someone asks for a simple change that can easily be resolved. If it is legal and doable, do it. Make the effort.

I am happy to report on at least one policing success story. It started out as a horror show and every cop's nightmare. Camden, New Jersey is the 12th largest city in N.J. and acts as the county seat. It has been fighting an uphill battle for decades. Only a few years ago Camden gained the notorious title of "Most Dangerous City in America". The City went broke in 2012 and laid off half the Police Force that was said to be corrupt and recalcitrant. After a record number of murders, they disbanded the rest of the Department and formed a new regional

Camden County Metro Police Department based upon the foundation of Community Policing.[220]

They shifted the paradigm by taking the cops out of cars and from behind desks. They put many Officers on bikes and issued this directive: Treat the people you engage, like citizens, not suspects. They attempted to make the worst nine square miles of New Jersey more tolerable. They wanted the cops to care whether a person lived or died.[221]

Six years later Camden is now looked upon as a potential national model for Community Policing. They have drastically reduced violent crime by flooding the streets with beat cops. They went from a force of 200 to 400, hiring back 3/4 of the old Force. The downside was they hired Officers at a lower salary and with less benefits than the City Force originally had. Mayor Moran stated, "We don't talk about defunding the Police, we talk about re-appropriating resources, making sure our Officers are fit with the right equipment to do their daily job, but more importantly well-trained, and training never ends."[222]

Besides the fact that the NJ State Supreme Court ruled that it was illegal to disband the original Police Force (it was too late because the new Department was already running because the judicial system is slow and also sucks), and the NAACP felt the new Force wasn't diverse enough but the Camden County Metro Police Department was off and running. Some residents complained that the new Force was aggressive regarding petty offenses.[223] This is a return to the old *Broken Windows* method of policing. It still works today.

The broken windows theory is a criminological theory that states that visible signs of crime, anti-social behavior, and civil disorder create an urban environment that encourages further crime and disorder, including serious crimes. The theory suggests that policing methods that target minor crimes such as vandalism, loitering, public drinking,

---

[220] Editorial, *"Camden is proof police can change their ways"* The Star Ledger, (April 9, 2017), n.p.

[221] Ibid

[222] Joe Atmonavage, *"Lessons from a city that embraced police reform"* The Star Ledger, (June 11,2020), Pg. 1

[223] Ibid.

jaywalking and fare evasion help to create an atmosphere of order and lawfulness, thereby preventing more serious crimes.

The theory was introduced in a 1982 article by social scientists James Q. Wilson and George L. Kelling. It was further popularized in the 1990s by New York City Police Commissioner William Bratton and Mayor Rudy Giuliani, whose policing policies were influenced by the theory.[224] Together they brough New York City back.

It has been six years and they are still working out the kinks at the CCMPD. Change will not come overnight, and there are still a lot of other social issues to address like poverty, but they are moving forward. This model Police Department flies in the face of the Defund the Police Movement. They increased the size of their Force while stressing more and better training. That's how to get positive results. These other cities on the other side of progress have subscribed to General Patton's quote, "A good plan violently executed now is better than a perfect plan executed next week." They want to defund or eliminate their local Police Department and replace them with social workers immediately. This is a violently executed plan that will get many innocent people hurt. Everyone needs to slow down and look at other options like the CCMPD model. There should be no rush to eliminate a Police Department. In addition to the defund movement, there is another growing movement to humiliate the Officers themselves. This is not your classic carrot and the stick approach. There is absolutely no carrot as a reward and the stick is used to beat the shit out of an already dead horse. One example has now been implemented by the Union County Prosecutor's Office. As of June 22, 2020 the UCPO will disclose the names of future and retroactive investigative employees who were subjected to major discipline, going back at least 10 years. Instances include underlying misconduct:

- Involved in deception, theft or dishonesty.
- Demonstrated a bias toward a particular race, ethnicity, religion, gender, identity, sexual preference, or other group.

---

[224] https://en.wikipedia.org/wiki/Broken_windows_theory

- Pertained to excessive use of force and/or criminal act of violence.
- Touched upon an investigation and/or prosecution of a crime. This would include, but not be limited to, mishandling of evidence, mishandling of falsification of official reports/records, improper conduct relevant to a confidential source/informant, or conduct negatively impacting trustful testimony.
- Reflected an abuse of their positions as a public employee and/or sworn member of law enforcement. This would include, but is not limited to, abuses of power and misuses of public property and/or paid time.[225]

I have nothing against properly distributed and fair discipline and the resulting consequences. These listed offenses seem to be of a severity high enough to warrant instant termination as they demonstrate a complete disregard of the Oath of Office and their sworn duty to uphold it. Why would an agency retain an employee that has violated their oath and no longer has any credibility? How many times does someone have to lie to you before you consider them a liar? Any retention of such an employee would be a further breach of confidence of that same office and invite future law suits. Hence, a terminated employee who has already suffered his or her penalty (if not followed up by a criminal charge for such offenses), faces double jeopardy, as well as embarrassment (to be shared with their family) with further exposure (retroactive to 10 years). This serves no one any purpose and only rubs salt into an old wound. They absolutely should not be permitted to work in public service anywhere again. Personnel records like health records used to be secure (HIPAA) and confidential. Now nothing is sacred.

Law enforcement agencies across the Country should work to improve their operations. They should follow already successful examples. They should move to terminate the dead wood, the lazy, the corrupt, the untrustworthy, or those plain unfit for the job. This will

---

[225] Union County, *"Prosecutor's Office to disclose names of disciplined investigative employees"* Union County Local Source, (July 2, 2020), Pg. 1

require major concessions in employee contracts. It should not take years to remove a person from law enforcement who should not be working there today. The good of the many! Departments should also improve their methods on how they care for their Officers. They should start with a comprehensive recruitment process that also includes an in-depth mental screening. There should be annual physical as well as mental capability tests that Officers must pass. There is talk of making law enforcement positions a licensing profession. I agree with this but, the Department has to make available the resources for the Officer to improve and maintain their status with Continuing Education Units (CEU) or other training. Everyone always wants everything but it is still all about the Benjamins. You get what you pay for. If you pay for a SEAL, then you get a SEAL! You pay less, you get less. The New Jersey Basic Course for Police Officers that governs the 16 Academies across the state is 259 pages. It needs to be 500 pages.[226] The public wants a watchful and caring guardian that does the job of a hardened fearless warrior, but they want enough plausible deniability for themselves so they don't have to see the ugly part of the job. They want the Police to fight the evil that they themselves deny exists. They want law and order until they get pulled over for speeding. They want the bad guys brought to justice until they get a call from the Police Station that their child is in custody. They want to be the content sheep that live in peace, but they don't want to know anything about how the Sheep Dog fends off the wolf. I am totally for reminding Officers and the public that law enforcement is a profession and it should contain professionals. There should be set standards across the board to have a common benchmark for all Officers to meet. In a world where it seems that many people want to bend or change the rules to fit their personal agenda, baseball Coach John Scolinos, explained it in his lecture, *Don't Widen the Plate,* from 17 inches to accommodate someone that can't throw over it. The player needs to meet the set standard. (A recommended and short read)

---

[226]   Karen Stahl, *"Jersey Knows Best, Why NJ Cops are the best of the best-trained"* New Jersey Cops, (Aug 2020), pg. 33

"If I am lucky," Coach Scolinos concluded, *"you will remember one thing from this old coach today. It is this: if we fail to hold ourselves to a higher standard, a standard of what we know to be right; if we fail to hold our spouses and our children to the same standards, if we are unwilling or unable to provide a consequence when they do not meet the standard; and if our schools and churches and our government fail to hold themselves accountable to those they serve, there is but one thing to look forward to ...* "With that, he held home plate in front of his chest, turned it around, and revealed its dark black backside." *... dark days ahead."*[227] There has to be investigations to keep a check on the warriors but they need to remove Internal Affairs Investigations from within the individual Departments for more serious offenses. The public no longer trusts Departments to police themselves. Some have even questioned the County Prosecutor's Offices regarding these investigations because everyone knows everyone. What's left? A civilian review board that has no working knowledge of Police Operations? The New Jersey Supreme Court has recently decided a civilian review board in Newark can provide oversight to the City's Police Department, but does not have subpoena power or the ability to investigate internal affairs.[228] They need to work on this one until they come up with a palatable solution. It wasn't long ago that Police were held in high regard by the public. They were heroes at 9/11 and again moving into the pandemic. Then One Big Pile Of Shit turned the tide against them. It will take some time for this to even out and right itself to a normal condition once again.

---

[227] Chris Sperry, Baseball/Life.LLC
[228] Katie Sobko, *"NJ Supreme Court rules Newark civilian board can provide police oversight — within limits"* NorthJersey.com,)Aug. 19,2020)

Chapter Twenty-Two

Self-Reflection

"I would choose no other life than the life I have had
and no other death than the one we go to."

- C.S. Lewis, The Last Battle

My Ethics Class has taken up a good amount of my time over the past 20 years, in my heart as well as in my brain. The course originally ran the entire recruit day of five hours (after PT). As more requirements were pushed onto the Academy, the Director (not an asshole) was nice enough to allow me to retain a half day. I chose the morning session as that was a 3-hour block as opposed to after lunch that would have only provided me with 2 hours and sleepier recruits. I always brought enough material for a few days (as you can see) and always struggled to get to the point in my abbreviated schedule.

I needed to constantly updated the material as time flew by, and I realized the recruits were getting younger every year. All my original examples meant nothing to them. Viet Nam was as relevant as the Civil

War. O.J. Simpson had been long forgotten and Rodney King could have been a fairy tale.

When I was on the job, my morning routine consisted of the following. My alarm would often surprise me as if I didn't know it were going to go off (even though my OCD had forced me to check it at least three times the night before). As I hit the bathroom, I would flick on the radio to get the local traffic news. My City lay between Route 24 and Route 78. If there was a bad wreck, that would mean my day was off to a crappy start because the traffic would be backed up into my jurisdiction and my Officers may be tied up assisting the Troopers.

Showered and dressed, I would pick up the newspaper from the front walk and check the headline to make sure the name of my City was not the news of the day. Okay to proceed to breakfast. I would quickly scan through the paper and not find any other bad news that would impact me directly. However, I might come across a story about a friend or acquaintance from another Department. By the time I reached the local section, if my name had not yet popped up, I only had one more thing to examine and that was the obituary. If I were absent from the carefully alphabetized list, I was good to go to work.

If I had found any articles regarding Police misdeeds, I would highlight the front page to remind me to cut it out at the end of the day. I would also circle the particular article within the paper. My wife would enter the kitchen and see me vigorously coloring in the paper and she would say, "What did they do this time?" She was well aware of my routine and the almost guaranteed possibility that the cops had screwed up once again or been accused of something they either, did or did not do.

It was disheartening when I read about someone that I knew. The first person to fall was my own PT instructor, not long after my Police Academy days. He was an Officer from a nearby Department within the County. I never learned the back story as to how he became involved, but he was arrested for selling drugs. You couldn't have picked a nicer guy. One other person in my Academy class was arrested some years later for credit card fraud. He on the other hand, was a dick right from the start. Sometimes, there is Karma.

It didn't matter if I knew the Officer in the article or on the news segment on tv, or if he or she was someone from another state across the country. It was always sad and disappointing when someone befell the radioactive like impact from OBPOS because it would tarnish all the other badges worn by all the rest of dedicated hard-working Officers. I never lost any sleep over the racist, the hateful, the brutal, the extremely stupid, and especially not the criminal. I spent over twenty years trying to save those that were worth saving or at least made an attempt to save themselves.

My last few years of my Law Enforcement career were spent as Patrol Bureau Commander. My Department had 51 sworn officers when I was appointed in 1977. The numbers dropped into the forties when they decided to go to civilian dispatchers, eliminating several sworn Officers by attrition. This sounds like a small department but the CBS Interactive Business Network reported that 87 percent of all Police Departments in the United States have just a few dozen Officers in their Force. That made us a medium sized Department. Citizens of the northeastern U.S. know of only two Police Departments to make comparisons to: Mayberry consisting of the beloved Sheriff and his zany Deputy, and the NYPD, that is an entire army of approximately 35,000 to 40,000 strong.

When I started in 1977, I was badge number 51. I retired in 2004 as the 3rd senior member of the Department. In total, I have worked with approximately 117 officers in my Department (I may have missed one or two here or there). During my 28 years:

- 13 officers left the department for various reasons (11%)
- 16 left for other police jobs (14%) My Sergeant with the Lone Ranger silver bullets always said, "The grass is always greener on the other side of the fence util you have to mow it."
- 4 left on early medical retirement (3%)
- 4 died (4%)
- 37 officers did not finish a 25-year career with the same Department. (32%)

On more than one occasion over my career an Officer in my Department received the proverbial tap on the shoulder and asked to leave for one reason or the other. In most instances we never knew the circumstances and often didn't know what happened until the Officer was already gone.

I usually had about 100 recruits in my class and asked a third of them to stand. I explain to them that this is a representative number of people that may not complete 25-years of service. It is not as easy as it may sound to go to work, do your job, not screw up, and go home safe at the end of the day.

I understood the importance of Community Policing early on, although the term had not yet become the flavor of the month in law enforcement circles. I had run the Crime Prevention Unit for ten years and was intrinsically involved with the public on many levels. I came out with a few directives as Lieutenant, some popular, some not. (Remember I got blamed for one that was not mine) I asked my Officers to turn their AM/FM radios down and open the patrol car window year-round so they could hear what was going on. One of my requests to Patrol Officers was for them to meet at least one person a day not associated with a call for service. That meant that they had to physically get their stationary cop asses out of their car and approach someone to say hello in a non-threatening situation. This wasn't as easy as it sounds. The first hurdle to overcome was that cops become very sedentary and unmotivated if not required to move. The second being, that the public gets nervous when Police approach them. An unfunny line they *always* said when a Police Officer approached them was, "I didn't do it." Never funny.

My City was referred to as an upscale suburban bedroom community. This meant that there were a lot of well-to-do people that commuted to NYC. With the kids in school, the streets were not teeming with people. You would probably see more landscapers on any given day than residents. I tried to motivate my Officers so they would not easily fall into the complacent, uncaring mode.

I started the Bicycle Patrol, that literally, took me twelve years to get rolling (no pun intended). I laid the grown work with the first Chief and was winning him over up right up until the day he retired. I restarted my campaign with the next Chief, and he also seemed receptive right up to the day he dropped dead of heart attack. I figured that third time was a charm but number three had absolutely no interest (in anything). It was an uphill battle. So much so that the Deputy Chief literally ordered me not to say the word bicycle (absolutely true – progress through aggravation). I told you cops hate change.

I finally managed to get the Administration to come around and the bike patrol was a huge success. The Officers who said they weren't going to wear shorts, witnessed how happy and comfortable the Bike Officers were. The Unit grew to nine Officers and the bicycle patrol hating Chief always managed to get his picture on the front page of the local paper standing next to them. Of course, I was not in any of the photos. I didn't need to be because I was proud of my Officers and the job they were doing.

Bike Patrol was a perfect fit for the D.A.R.E officers because it was easier to work them into a bicycle patrol schedule after their classes at the schools. One Officer said, "They pay me to ride a bike and exercise while I'm working, you can't beat that." I was happy to see the local Volunteer First Aid Squad start their own bike unit for events and large crowds. There were occasions when the Bike Officers would beat the patrol car to the scene.

What does a bike patrol have to do with ethics? Community Policing, public relations, whatever you call it, is crucial to both the Police and the public (Camden found out the hard way). If you don't have the support of the community it makes a tough job ten times harder. We had a walking beat (24/7/365) for the Central Business District and that was a nice extra the Department provided to the taxpayers. It finally became cost prohibitive because the Officer(s) were geographically limited to their response. They were also limited as to the equipment that they could carry. I have said this before, "It's all about the money."

In my Department I was not the smartest, the dumbest, the strongest, the weakest, the tallest, the shortest, the fastest, the slowest, the best shot, the worst shot, or the bravest. I started my classes telling the recruits I was also not the most ethical person in the room, but the material I presented made me strive to be that person. The articles I cut out of the newspaper were a constant reminder to me of what I had signed up to do. I got the protect part right away. We were the Sheep Dogs watching over the flock keeping them safe from the wolves. It took me some time before I understood the serve part. At first I hated the Public Servant moniker. I was nobody's servant. I finally grasped what the service was. It was holding the trust of the public. It was being fair to everyone. It was helping everyone, even the people I arrested. One of my most proud moments was when the drug dealer had asked me to be his reference. There was never anything personal. I was rooting for him. Another guy that I had arrested recently friended me on Facebook.

As a young rookie I was walking my post and the wannabe gang members had been sitting on a front stoop of a building. Someone tossed a bottle at me that missed me by a few feet. I calmly walked up to the group and asked them if they wanted to try it again because they had lousy aim at a distance. No one took me up on my offer. I sat down with them and explained the situation. I was the designated good-guy and if they chose to break the law, it was my job to arrest them. I made no threats. I stated the facts. They fully understood, and thereafter we had a relationship much like in the Roadrunner & Coyote cartoon. At the end of the day we would punch out on the clock and say good night. Sometimes we would resume our jobs and pick up the very next day right where we had left off.

On another occasion I witnessed a drug transaction right in front of me. I was sitting in an "unmarked car" that any five-year old would recognize as a Police Car. I couldn't let it go, on the grounds of basic stupidity. I called for backup to take the seller and I would grab the buyer. Backup arrived and I got into a very physical confrontation with my suspect. I finally subdued, handcuffed him, and transported him to HQ. As we both sat panting at my desk, I said to him, "Alex, we're getting too old for this shit." He agreed and we had a good laugh about it.

I would often assist the defendants with their case, not in a legal way, but by using common sense. I would absolutely tell them if they needed a lawyer or what else they may need to make the best case or get the best deal for themselves.

Every day you should meet someone, not just interact with them. That means you need to remember their name for the next time you see them.

Every day you should help someone, not because it is your job, but because you want to.

Every day you should look people in the eye, because they deserve to be seen.

Every day you should listen to people, because they deserve to be heard.

Every day you should help someone, not because you have to, but because they need your help.

In one of the last scenes in the 1998 movie, Private Ryan, Captain John Miller (played by Tom Hanks), lies dying after the heroic battle to hold the town against the Nazis. He turns to Private Ryan and tells him, "Earn this, earn it!" Everyone, not just Law Enforcement Officers, needs to earn it every day.

One thing that startled me when I was perusing the newspapers for tales of unethical behavior was the obituary posts of retired Police Officers. While the killing of an active duty Officer always made front page news and was followed by an elaborate funeral, the retired Officers barely occupied a couple inches of print. The really surprising aspect of these obituaries was the fact that the Officers may have worked 25, 30, or even 40 years in law enforcement and it hardly registered a mention in the column. Often the description recounting a long and distinguished career rated less words than the years on the job. A common line would state, "Mr. Jones was a Police Officer in X Township for 27 years before retiring in 1998." That's it!. No extra details of the person's service are provided. No mention of lives saved or changed for the better. No awards or accolades. No honors or sparkling review of an amazing decades long career fighting the fight against evil.

This glaring omission of information led me to the understanding that we as Police Officers think it is all about the job while we are doing it. It really isn't. It is about the way we live our lives while doing the job. Another important factor is that people have many lives. Some of them are consecutive as we grow from toddler to teenager to adult. These are all separate periods where we do and learn specific things and advance and develop in different ways.

Multiple lives we live are concurrent with each other. We have varied roles as a family member; brother, sister, parent, child, grandparent, and many other relationships. Then we have a work life that requires an entirely different set of demands and responsibilities. Within law enforcement it is the same growing pattern starting with rookie to Patrol Officer to possibly a supervisor or special assignment. Again, each category you fall into requires a completely different set of tools, expectations ad responsibilities while you are still living your personal life at the same time. It is almost impossible to be the same person in all of our lives. We need to be different people in order to accomplish our goals. We can however, be a decent, caring, and fair person in all of these roles. We cannot lose sight of out true person inside of us. Life is too short. I encourage you to read the poem by Linda Ellis entitled *The Dash*.[229] She describes how the dash in between your birth and death dates on your tombstone is what matters. Live the dash in your life to the best of your ability.

The True Test of Your Character Begins Now... When No one Sees!

Class Dismissed.

I do solemnly swear (or affirm) that I will support the Constitution of the United States and the Constitution of the State of New Jersey, and that I will bear true faith and allegiance to the same and to the Governments established in the United States and in this State, County and Municipality, under the authority of the people; and that I will faithfully, impartially and justly perform all the duties of the office of Police Officer according to the best of my ability. So help me God.[230]

---

[229] *The Dash* © 1996-2020 Southwestern Inspire Kindness, Inc. All Rights Reserved. By Linda Ellis, Copyright © 2020 Inspire Kindness, thedashpoem.com
[230] www.njleg.state.nj.us>bills, Section 1 of P.L.1951, c.351 (C.41:2A-6).

Acknowledgements

I would first like to express my appreciation to the people and instructors at The Center for American and International Law (CAIL). They laid the foundation for this class so many years ago. I retained some of their basic format to build upon but had to improvise as the decades passed to stay current and relevant for the recruits. Those instructors must have made a big impact upon me for me to pick up their teachings and run with it for another twenty years. I believed in their words and what they were trying to say. It became much more to me. It started out as a simple message of do the right thing that transformed into a survival guide on how to save your career, your reputation, your family, and possibly your life. Their message struck a chord deep within me that I could possibly help others get through or hopefully, avoid altogether, a difficult situation. I hope they can forgive me for going *slightly* off the rails to push the ethics message.

I would like to thank my co-instructors, Lt. Stephen Wilde and Chief Doug Marvin, for getting me through the tough beginning. Chief Marvin held on as long as he could until requirements of a higher position pulled him away. After all those crazy years, we remain friends.

I would like to once again express my appreciation to Chief Eric Mason, Director of the John H. Stamler Academy, for fitting me into an already tight schedule. His professionalism and good humor always made my days of instruction something to look forward to. His staff was absolutely great and always had my thousands of hand-outs ready for me upon my arrival. The AV crew prepared my equipment and the drill instructor struck just the right amount of fear into the recruits so that they paid attention and stayed awake (for the most part).

Last and certainly not least, my wife Cindy has put up with me for way longer than humans should have to endure. She allowed me to color in the newspaper at the breakfast table like a five-year-old with a Cracker Barrel kid menu and then make swiss cheese out of it, gathering all my current stories of misdeeds. She spent many nights editing my hodgepodge of misplaced commas and hyphens so that my readers could understand what it was I was trying to say. My family has survived an entire police career while maintaining most of our sanity at the same time. Not an easy task.

About The Author

Robert D'Ambola has spent over 45 years involved in law enforcement, emergency management and corporate security. This is Robert's fifth book. His first two; Shut Up When You Talk to Me and Just Plain Stupid, are a collection of short but unbelievable true stories. His third book was a work of fiction based upon real events. Knights of the Forest tells the tale of a small band of boys growing up in simpler times during the 60s. He branched out with This is Not Your Mother's Cookbook, which is really not a cook book. This forth book included some of his favorite (unhealthy) foods accompanied by humorous stories.

He holds a BA in Law/Justice from Glassboro State College (Rowan University), a Master's Degree in Administrative Science from Fairleigh Dickinson University and graduated from the Northwestern University School of Police Staff & Command. Robert held many ranks in the Police Department including Detective Sergeant, Traffic Lieutenant, and finally Patrol Commander. He was assigned to the Union County Narcotics Strike Force and Union/Essex Auto Theft Task Force. The latter assignment was during the period when Newark, New Jersey held the dubious honor of "Stolen Car Capital of the World." Robert remains a certified Instructor by the New Jersey Police Training Commission and has taught at the John H. Stamler Police Academy for over 30 years, the last 23 as the Ethics Instructor for all Police Recruit classes that passes through their doors.

After retiring from the force, Robert became Chief of Security, Certified Business Continuity Professional & Emergency Planner for a global publishing company. His office was directly on the Hudson River waterfront with a front row seat of the New York skyline. It was here Robert was able to witness the "Miracle on the Hudson" when on January 15, 2009, US Airways jetliner, flight 1549 was forced down into the frigid Hudson River directly outside his office building. He later was Director of Security for an urban hospital and then moved on to work with one of the top Healthcare Networks in the country as an investigator and instructor.